the
rom-com
cookbook

the
rom-com
cookbook

ROMANTIC-COMEDY-INSPIRED RECIPES THAT WILL
MAKE THEM SAY, "I'LL HAVE WHAT SHE'S HAVING"

BY TARA THEOHARIS WITH KRISTEN MULROONEY
ILLUSTRATIONS BY SARAH LONG

INSIGHT
EDITIONS

SAN RAFAEL · LOS ANGELES · LONDON

CONTENTS

➤——————➤ ♥ ◄——————◄

CHAPTER FIVE: THE HOLIDAYS

CHAPTER SIX: THE BREAKUP AND MAKEUP

CHAPTER SEVEN: HAPPILY EVER AFTER

INTRODUCTION

A good meal is like the perfect partner—it leaves you satisfied, you could have it every night, and you can't wait to show it off to your friends. In this book, I hope to introduce you to your next great love. Whether you're a cute-but-clumsy editor of a fashion magazine who's never touched their kitchen, a cute-but-clumsy bakery owner, or merely a cute-but-clumsy fan of love stories and groan-worthy puns, there's a recipe for you within these pages.

Romantic comedies can make you laugh, cry, and see yourself in the characters; they'll also make you wish you had a larger, more colorful wardrobe. Above all else, rom-coms know what they are. They deliver just what you want and give you an ending to cheer for. They're there for you when you need a moment of comfort, and this book is the same. These recipes, inspired by moments in some of my favorite movies, will bring you joy and comfort as you follow the simple-to-understand instructions.

So put on your cutest apron, play some sweet tunes, and make something delicious, whether it's for yourself, a perfect date, or a festive dinner party. Consider me the sassy best friend with the good advice: I'll walk you through each step, and if you need some extra help, you can check out the glossary, conversions, and other tips and tricks in the back.

The book is broken down into the stages of a relationship: In "Meat-Cute," you'll find meat dishes ranging from appetizers to full meals. "Let's Meet for Drinks" shakes up some cocktail ideas, followed by "The Morning After" to help soak up that hangover with some delicious breakfast dishes. "Long-Term Relationship," offers entrees for your next dinner at home. Once you're committed, don't forget "The Holidays," an ode to our favorite holiday rom-coms and the festive foods they include. But if the relationship doesn't last, it leads to "The Breakup and Makeup," featuring all the desserts you'll want to binge in your pajamas. That's followed, of course, by "Happily Ever After," a collection of sweet and savory recipes inspired by some of our favorite rom-com endings. Finally, join me at "The After Party" for suggestions on how to bring these recipes together for your next gathering.

Rom-com fans know it's nearly impossible to change your partner, but I'm here to tell you that you *can* change the recipes in this book. Read through them as written, then feel free to substitute ingredients to make the recipe meat free, dairy free, gluten free, or alcohol free. Add an extra few cloves of garlic. Top everything with a scoop of ice cream. Whatever makes it perfect just for you.

I hope you love this book as much as you love the movies that inspired it. Now get out there and find your dream meal!

—TARA THEOHARIS

Timeline of Films

Roman Holiday
1953

White Christmas
1954

Breakfast at Tiffany's
1961

Sixteen Candles
1984

Dirty Dancing
1987

Moonstruck
1987

The Princess Bride
1987

The Mirror Has Two Faces
1996

Clueless
1995

Sleepless in Seattle
1993

Groundhog Day
1993

Pretty Woman
1990

When Harry Met Sally
1989

Mystic Pizza
1988

Cocktail
1988

My Best Friend's Wedding
1997

The Wedding Singer
1998

You've Got Mail
1998

10 Things I Hate About You
1999

Notting Hill
1999

She's All That
1999

Amélie
2001

How to Lose a Guy in 10 Days
2003

My Big Fat Greek Wedding
2002

The Wedding Planner
2001

Serendipity
2001

Legally Blonde
2001

Bridget Jones's Diary
2001

Love Actually
2003

13 Going on 30
2004

50 First Dates
2004

Hitch
2005

The 40-Year-Old Virgin
2005

Wedding Crashers
2005

Last Holiday
2006

The Break-Up
2006

Eat Pray Love
2010

The Proposal
2009

It's Complicated
2009

Forgetting Sarah Marshall
2008

27 Dresses
2008

Enchanted
2007

The Holiday
2006

Bridesmaids
2011

About Time
2013

The Spirit of Christmas
2015

A Christmas Prince: The Royal Wedding
2018

Crazy Rich Asians
2018

The Princess Switch
2018

Your Place or Mine
2023

Red, White & Royal Blue
2023

The Lost City
2022

To All the Boys: P.S. I Still Love You
2020

Holidate
2020

Always Be My Maybe
2019

chapter
one

MEAT-CUTE

You're at your local butcher shop buying ingredients for your usual dinner-for-one when you and another shopper accidentally grab the same salami. How awkward! The two of you stumble through some salami-based double entendres before realizing, when you finally lock eyes, that you're staring at the most gorgeous person you've ever seen. Congratulations, you've just had a meet-cute—or, more accurately, a *meat*-cute. How exhilarating! If you see an increase in candlelit meals in your future, these meat dishes are perfect for celebrating those serendipitous moments that turn your nightly dinner-for-one into dinner-for-two (or more).

WHAT SHE'S HAVING

Inspired by: *When Harry Met Sally*

Can men and women be friends? Of course! A man and a woman can find plenty of things to do together where the sex part won't get in the way. Having lunch, for instance. What could possibly be sexy about a nice turkey sandwich? Sure, the Russian dressing might make you moan softly. And the moan might become louder and faster, growing with each bite. Yes! Oh, and those pickles, the pickles!—YES! "More!" you'll shout. "More coleslaw!" you'll shout, until your head falls back and, as quickly as you've started, you're finished. Take inspiration from Sally Albright and create this drool-worthy version of what she's having. You won't have to fake your excitement.

COLESLAW:

2 tablespoons mayonnaise

½ tablespoon granulated sugar

2 teaspoons lemon juice

1½ teaspoons vinegar

⅛ teaspoon salt

⅛ teaspoon freshly ground black pepper

3 ounces (⅔ cup) shredded cabbage

2 tablespoons grated carrot

SANDWICH:

2 slices white bread

½ tablespoon Russian dressing

½ pound sliced deli turkey

2 long pickle slices

TO MAKE THE COLESLAW:

1. In a large bowl, whisk together the mayonnaise, sugar, lemon juice, vinegar, salt, and pepper. Add the cabbage and carrot to the bowl and mix together. Set aside.

TO MAKE THE SANDWICH:

2. Toast the white bread and slather one side of one slice with the Russian dressing.

3. Carefully stack all the turkey on top of the dressing-covered slice of bread.

4. Place the pickle slices on top of the turkey, and then top with ¼ cup of coleslaw.

5. Cover the sandwich with the other piece of bread, and slice in half.

Don't have premade Russian dressing? Make your own! Whisk together ¼ cup mayonnaise, ½ tablespoon grated onion, 1 teaspoon chili sauce, 1 teaspoon minced dill pickle, ½ teaspoon lemon juice, ½ teaspoon grated horseradish, ¼ teaspoon Worcestershire sauce, and paprika, salt, and pepper to taste.

Rosie's Meatballs

Inspired by: *The Wedding Singer*

Here's the secret to fifty years of growing old with someone: It's in the meatballs. Sweet old Rosie's meatballs are so good, they're practically their own currency, and you can make your own with this perfect "Grandma's been cooking all day" recipe that's worth its weight in gold. Let these savory meatballs simmer during your singing lesson and have them ready by dinnertime. You'll be tempted to eat them by the handful (but make sure they've cooled down)!

SAUCE:

2 tablespoons olive oil

½ cup yellow onion, minced (about ½ onion)

6 cloves garlic, minced

6 ounces tomato paste

6 ounces water

Two 28-ounce cans crushed tomatoes

1 tablespoon sugar

1½ teaspoons kosher salt

½ teaspoon freshly ground black pepper

1 tablespoon fresh basil, chopped

1 pinch red pepper flakes

MEATBALLS:

¾ cups breadcrumbs

½ cup whole milk

1 pound ground beef

1 pound ground pork

½ cup yellow onion, minced (about ½ onion)

3 cloves garlic, minced

2 eggs, slightly beaten

¼ cup Parmesan cheese, grated

1 teaspoon kosher salt

½ teaspoon freshly ground black pepper

1 tablespoon fresh basil, chopped

1 tablespoon fresh parsley, chopped

TO MAKE THE SAUCE:

1. Place the olive oil in a large pot over medium-high heat and add the onions. Sauté until the onions are transparent, 2 to 3 minutes, and then add the minced garlic. Cook for 2 minutes.

2. Add the tomato paste, water, crushed tomatoes, sugar, salt, pepper, basil, and red pepper flakes. Bring to a boil and then reduce the heat to low and let simmer for 15 minutes or until the meatballs are ready. (It will continue to simmer while the meatballs cook in the sauce.)

TO MAKE THE MEATBALLS:

3. Cover a baking sheet with aluminum foil and set aside.

4. In a large bowl, mix together the breadcrumbs and milk and let sit on the side for 10 minutes, or until the breadcrumbs have soaked up the liquid. While waiting for that to soak, move the top rack in your oven to the highest tier and preheat the oven on the "broil" setting.

5. In the bowl with the breadcrumb mixture, place the beef, pork, onion, garlic, eggs, Parmesan cheese, salt, pepper, basil, and parsley and mix with your hands until thoroughly combined.

6. Form the meat mixture into 2-inch balls, or about the size of the inside of your palm.

7. Place the meatballs on the prepared baking sheet and place in the broiler. Cook for 3 minutes or until browned, and then flip the meatballs to the other side. Cook for another 3 minutes or until browned and able to be moved without falling apart.

8. Place the browned meatballs in the sauce and simmer on low for 1 hour.

9. Place the meatballs and sauce on a plate for serving. Take a big bite and enjoy!

YIELD: 16 MEATBALLS
PREP TIME: 30 MINUTES
COOK TIME: 1 HOUR

MY BIG FAT GREEK "~~MOOSECACA~~" MOUSSAKA

Inspired by: *My Big Fat Greek Wedding*

Though the uncultured may laugh when Toula Portokalos brings a container of "moosecaca" to school, anyone familiar with moussaka would be drooling and asking for a bite. Make this traditional Greek casserole featuring eggplant, lamb, and béchamel for any gathering, and the Greeks will think you're part of the family. (Just please don't serve with a side of Windex.) καλή όρεξη!

MOUSSAKA FILLING:

Oil, for greasing

2 large eggplants, cut lengthwise into ½-inch-thick slices

1 tablespoon plus 1 teaspoon kosher salt, divided

3 tablespoons olive oil, divided

1 pound ground lamb

1 yellow onion, diced

3 cloves garlic, minced

One 8-ounce can tomato sauce

1 teaspoon ground cinnamon

1 teaspoon dried oregano

¼ teaspoon freshly ground black pepper

BÉCHAMEL SAUCE:

¼ cup salted butter

4 tablespoons all-purpose flour

2 cups whole milk

¼ teaspoon ground nutmeg

1 egg yolk

¼ cup Parmesan cheese, grated

TO MAKE THE MOUSSAKA FILLING:

1. Preheat the oven to 350°F. Grease a 9-by-13-inch casserole dish with oil and set aside. Line a plate with a paper towel and set aside.

2. Place the eggplant slices on a large baking sheet and sprinkle with 1 tablespoon of kosher salt. Set aside. They will release water while you prepare the other ingredients.

3. Place 1 tablespoon of olive oil in a large skillet and heat over medium-high heat for 1 minute. Add the lamb to the skillet and cook for 5 to 7 minutes, stirring often, until browned. Remove the lamb and set aside in a medium bowl.

4. Place the onions and garlic in the skillet and sauté on medium-high heat for 2 to 3 minutes or until the onions are transparent and the mixture is fragrant.

5. Add the tomato sauce, cinnamon, oregano, remaining 1 teaspoon salt, and the pepper to the skillet. Return the cooked lamb to the skillet and mix everything together. Bring to a simmer, then reduce the heat to medium-low and continue to simmer for 20 minutes. While the moussaka filling simmers, make the béchamel sauce.

TO MAKE THE BÉCHAMEL SAUCE:

6. Melt the butter in a small saucepan over medium heat. Stir in the flour until fully combined and nutty brown in color. Slowly add the milk, whisking constantly until it thickens into a sauce, 6 to 8 minutes. Remove the saucepan from heat, add the nutmeg, egg yolk, and Parmesan, and mix until thoroughly combined. Set aside.

7. Place the remaining 2 tablespoons olive oil in a large pan over medium-high heat.

8. Press the eggplant slices gently to remove any excess water, then pat dry with a paper towel. Working in batches so each slice sits flat in the pan, place the eggplant slices in the pan and cook for 2 minutes on each side, or until browned. Set the sautéed slices aside on the prepared plate.

9. Layer the ingredients in the casserole dish, starting with half the eggplant, all the meat sauce, the rest of the eggplant, and then the béchamel sauce on top.

10. Bake for 45 minutes or until the top becomes bubbly. Let cool and solidify for 15 minutes, then cut and serve. Moussaka keeps well in the refrigerator and makes for a delicious lunch the next day, hot or cold.

Prepare to Dine: Fezzik's Stew

Inspired by: *The Princess Bride*

When someone you care about is feeling under the weather, show your love with a little TLC. Tuck them into bed, tell them a story, and feed them something robust, like this tasty, comforting stew that works wonders when nursing someone back to health. Whether a member of your adventuring party is mostly dead, lost their feet below the ankles (and their hands at the wrist, their nose, tongue, and left eye followed by their right eye), or just looking for a little comfort, this cozy, hearty stew will have them feeling more than slightly alive in no time. Serve it to them just as they wish.

1 pound beef stew meat, cut into 1-inch cubes

2 tablespoons all-purpose flour

1½ teaspoons kosher salt, divided

1 teaspoon freshly ground black pepper, divided

2 tablespoons vegetable oil, divided

1 large yellow onion, roughly chopped

1 clove garlic, minced

4 cups beef broth

2 sprigs fresh thyme

1 bay leaf

1 teaspoon paprika

1 teaspoon Worcestershire sauce

4 large russet potatoes, peeled and cut into 1½- to 2-inch pieces

3 carrots, sliced into 1-inch pieces

1. Place the beef in a medium bowl and cover the meat with the flour, ½ teaspoon of salt, and ½ teaspoon of pepper. Mix together so all the meat is evenly coated.

2. Heat 1 tablespoon vegetable oil in a Dutch oven or large pot over medium-high heat. Add the beef pieces and cook for 5 minutes, or until browned on all sides but not cooked through. Remove the beef to a plate and set aside.

3. Heat the remaining 1 tablespoon of vegetable oil in the Dutch oven and add the onion and garlic, cooking for 3 minutes or until browned.

4. Add the beef, the remaining 1 teaspoon salt and ½ teaspoon of pepper, the beef broth, thyme sprigs, bay leaf, paprika, and Worcestershire sauce. Scrape up any browned bits from the bottom of the pot and mix everything together.

5. Bring to a boil, and then lower heat to medium-low and simmer, covered, for 1 hour.

6. Skim off any fat from the top with a cooking spoon and discard. Add the potatoes and carrots to the pot, mix, and then cover and simmer for another 40 minutes or until everything is tender.

7. Scoop into bowls and serve.

3 Lemon Centepiece-of-Chicken

Inspired by: *The Break-Up*

Sometimes the end of a relationship isn't caused by one big event, but rather a bunch of tiny things that build up until suddenly one last lemon breaks the camel's back. Gary had one job: Buy twelve lemons for the centerpiece Brooke was making for the beautiful dinner party she was single-handedly throwing for their families. But he couldn't even do that, coming home with just *three* lemons. The centerpiece was a no-go, but when life hands you *three* lemons, make chicken piccata. This creamy, citrusy dish will save any dinner party, even those that are full of petty arguments, crass jokes, and spontaneous groups singing a capella. Just make sure someone helps with the dishes at the end of the night.

2 skinless, boneless chicken breasts

1 teaspoon kosher salt

½ teaspoon freshly ground black pepper

½ cup all-purpose flour

3 tablespoons olive oil, divided

½ cup white wine

1 tablespoon capers, rinsed and drained

¼ cup salted butter, cut into cubes

2 tablespoons fresh lemon juice

1 teaspoon lemon zest

¼ cup heavy cream (can also use heavy whipping cream)

2 tablespoons chopped parsley, for garnish

1. Cut the chicken breasts in half horizontally, resulting in four pieces, and then place them between two sheets of parchment paper. Pound with a mallet until the breasts are about ½ inch thick.

2. In a small mixing bowl, combine the salt, pepper, and flour and dredge both sides of the chicken breast cutlets in the mixture.

3. In a large skillet over medium-high heat, heat 2 tablespoons of olive oil, and then fry the cutlets for 4 to 5 minutes or until browned. Flip and cook for another 4 minutes. Transfer the chicken to a plate.

4. Add the wine and capers to the skillet and bring to a boil, scraping up the brown bits from the pan and mixing together. Boil for 2 minutes or until the liquid has reduced, then add the butter, lemon juice, and lemon zest. Mix together and cook for another 2 minutes or until a sauce has formed. Stir in the heavy cream.

5. Add the chicken back into the skillet and cook for another 5 minutes, or until the chicken is cooked through.

6. Spoon the sauce on top of the chicken and serve with a sprinkle of parsley.

MARY'S LITTLE RACK OF LAMB

YIELD: 1 RACK OF LAMB
(2 TO 4 SERVINGS)
PREP TIME: 25 MINUTES
COOK TIME: 50 MINUTES
GF

Inspired by: *How to Lose a Guy in 10 Days*

Think it's easy to make someone fall in love with you in 10 days? Don't be so vain. You're going to have to follow Benjamin Barry's example and "pull out the big guns": a beautiful, cooked rack of lamb with cherry glaze. Pair with veggies, bread, red wine, and the NBA finals, and this is one bet you're sure to win. That is, unless your date doesn't eat meat . . .

LAMB:

1 teaspoon dried thyme

1 teaspoon dried rosemary

1 teaspoon kosher salt

½ teaspoon freshly ground black pepper

5 cloves garlic, minced, divided

1 rack of lamb (8 ribs, about 1½ pounds), frenched

2 tablespoons olive oil, divided

1 pound gold baby potatoes

3 carrots, bias cut in 1-inch slices

1 bunch asparagus, ends trimmed

CHERRY GLAZE:

1 shallot, minced

1 tablespoon olive oil

8 ounces frozen pitted cherries

1 cup red wine

1 cup chicken broth

1 tablespoon salted butter

TO MAKE THE LAMB:

1. Preheat the oven to 425°F. In a small bowl, mix the thyme, rosemary, salt, pepper, and half of the garlic.

2. Brush the rack of lamb with 1 tablespoon olive oil, and then sprinkle half of the seasoning mix all over the lamb. Set aside on a large plate.

3. Place the potatoes, carrot slices, and asparagus in a large Dutch oven and mix in the remaining 1 tablespoon of olive oil and the remaining seasoning mix. Remove the coated asparagus and set aside on a plate.

4. Cook the potatoes and carrots in the oven for 30 minutes, stirring once halfway through.

5. Mix the potatoes and carrots again and place the rack of lamb in the Dutch oven on top of the vegetables. Cook for 25 to 30 minutes or until the lamb is medium-rare (125°F). While the lamb is cooking, make the cherry glaze.

TO MAKE THE CHERRY GLAZE:

6. In a small saucepan over medium heat, sauté the shallot and remaining minced garlic in the olive oil for 1 minute. Add the cherries, wine, and chicken broth and bring to a boil. Cook for 5 to 8 minutes or until liquid is reduced by half. Stir in the butter and cook for another 2 minutes or until the glaze is thickened.

7. Allow the lamb to rest for 15 minutes, spoon the cherry glaze on top, and serve.

"DEATH ON A LEAF!"

Inspired by: *Hitch*

Basic principle: Pay attention to the details. What's your date wearing? What are they drinking? Has one side of their face swollen to three times its normal size? If the answer to that last question is yes, you're going to want to find some Benadryl STAT. Date doctor Alex "Hitch" Hitchens proves you can recover from any dating disaster after trying what he calls "Death on a Leaf," a bite-size version of Coquille St. Jacques. Make sure you know everyone's allergies before serving this impressive scallop dish, and have some antihistamines on hand, just in case. In the event of an emergency, your date will appreciate your attention to detail.

8 endive leaves

2 tablespoons salted butter

½ cup shallots, diced (about 1 to 2 shallots)

8 ounces white mushrooms, diced

¼ teaspoon kosher salt

¼ teaspoon freshly ground black pepper

1 cup white wine

1 pound scallops

2 tablespoons all-purpose flour

½ cup heavy cream (can also use heavy whipping cream)

1 egg yolk

½ teaspoon dried thyme

Zest of 1 lemon

¼ cup shredded Gruyère cheese

¼ cup breadcrumbs

1. Melt the butter in a large oven-safe pan over medium heat, then add the shallots. Sauté until translucent, about 3 minutes, and then add the mushrooms, salt, and pepper. Cook for 8 minutes or until the mushrooms are softened and browned.

2. Add the white wine to the pan and bring to a boil. Add the scallops to the pan and cook for 2 minutes on each side. Place the cooked scallops and mushrooms in a bowl, straining any additional liquid that came with them back into the pan. Set the bowl aside.

3. Add the flour to the pan with the leftover cooking liquid, stirring constantly for 1 minute over medium heat. Add the cream and bring to a boil. Cook for 10 minutes or until the liquid is reduced by half. Remove from the heat and whisk in the egg yolk quickly until fully combined. Mix in the thyme and lemon zest. Add the mushrooms and scallops back into the pan, then top with the shredded Gruyère and breadcrumbs. Broil for 2 minutes or until the cheese is melted and lightly browned.

4. Spoon equal portions of the scallop and mushroom mix onto the endive leaves and serve.

5. Place the endive leaves on a platter and set aside.

THE LOST CITY OF D(ELICIOUSNESS) CHARCUTERIE

Inspired by: *The Lost City*

Love is by far life's greatest adventure. Wait, no—life's greatest adventure is being kidnapped by a deranged millionaire and traipsing through an island jungle to make a perilous escape with a chiseled cover model. But after that, it's definitely love. Loretta Sage, writer of the Dr. Lovemore novels, is lucky enough to experience both when she's abducted by Abigail Fairfax and forced to help locate valuable treasure in the Lost City of D. And if that wasn't already adventure enough, Abigail also provides a charcuterie layout unlike any charcuterie you've ever seen before. Serve with Champagne and an offer the recipient literally cannot refuse.

1 lemon

1 orange

1 grapefruit

1 pint strawberries

1 pound cherries

Large bunch red grapes

1 pint golden berries

1 baguette French bread

8-ounce wheel of Brie

7-ounce wheel or wedge of Gouda with a red wax coating

8 slices cheddar cheese

8 large rectangular crackers

20 round butter crackers

16 savory square crackers

16 ounces sliced ham

8 ounces sliced salami

½ cup almonds

½ cup pistachios

½ cup dried banana chips

½ cup dried apricots

12 food-grade roses (yellow, red, and peach colored), (optional)

1. Line a large plate with paper towels. Rinse the lemon, orange, grapefruit, strawberries, cherries, grapes, and golden berries, and let them dry on the prepared plate.

2. Slice the lemon, orange, and grapefruit into thin rounds. Cut the grapes into smaller bunches.

3. Cut the French bread into ½-inch-thick slices.

4. Place the Brie, Gouda, and cheddar cheeses on opposite sides of the charcuterie board or table and pair with small cheese knives.

5. Fan out the crackers along the edges of the board and near the cheeses. Do the same with the slices of bread.

6. Place the grape bunches in different open spots on the board.

7. Roll the ham and salami slices and stack on top of one another in two separate spots of the board.

8. Add almonds and pistachios around the empty edges of the cheese.

9. Place small piles of banana chips and dried apricots near the center of the board.

10. Remove the stems from the roses and scatter the rose heads throughout the board, filling in any empty spots.

11. Place citrus rounds, strawberries, cherries, and golden berries throughout the board, sprinkling on top of the other food and arranging in any remaining empty spots.

chapter
two

LET'S MEET FOR DRINKS

You made it to happy hour! Girls, put on your flirtiest going out top.
Guys, go ahead and . . . oh, you're already set? How annoying. But,
anyway, the best time to find love is when you stop looking for it,
so forget about romance, grab your closest friends, and whip up
one of these fun cocktails to get the night started. Get out on the
dance floor, or maybe even on top of the bar, and don't be afraid to
let loose! When you're living a rom-com life, those embarrassing
moments can end up being the start of a beautiful relationship.

DIRTY MIXING: "I CARRIED A WATERMELON" COCKTAIL

Inspired by: *Dirty Dancing*

Everyone dreams of that perfect rom-com moment: You come face-to-face with a sexy stranger and effortlessly roll out a smooth opening line that instantly captivates them. Unfortunately, that dream usually plays out more like a nightmare, like when the tongue-tied Baby drops "I carried a watermelon" on the much older, much cooler Johnny Castle. Baby can't redo that awkward first impression, but at least she can repurpose the watermelon into something with a little more kick. This large cocktail will loosen your hips after just a few sips and have the whole party dirty dancing, and, like Baby and Johnny, you just might end the night with a time-of-your-life moment.

1 mini seedless watermelon
(about 3 to 5 pounds)

4 ounces lime juice
(about 2 large limes)

2 ounces simple syrup

3 ounces vodka

1. Slice off the top of a watermelon and hollow out the inside, saving the pulp.

2. Place the watermelon pulp in a blender and blend until smooth.

3. Strain through a sieve into a bowl, saving all the liquid (12 to 16 ounces), and discarding the remaining solids. Set aside.

4. Cut a thin slice from the bottom of the watermelon to allow it to stand up on its own. (Be careful not to cut deep enough to create a hole in the bottom.)

5. Add a handful of ice cubes, the watermelon juice, lime juice, simple syrup, and vodka to the hollowed-out watermelon. Stir together.

6. Place straws in the watermelon and enjoy!

Note: This recipe is gluten free if using a gluten-free vodka.

THE DING-A-LING

Inspired by: *Cocktail*

YIELD: 1 COCKTAIL
PREP TIME: 2 MINUTES
V, V+, GF*

Brian Flanagan's first attempt at bartending got off to a rocky start (what *is* in a martini?), but it didn't take long for him to become a pro. He can make all the standard cocktails with added flair (kamikaze, sex on the beach, and orgasm, for starters), plus he's got some unique drinks up his sleeve, including the Ding-a-Ling. This sweet-but-strong concoction will transport you to a busy '80s bar. For added flair, you can toss a shaker or spin a bottle while you're mixing this one, but don't worry if you can't master it—the world's last barman poet could tell you that sometimes the simple things are better than all the razzle-dazzle.

Ice cubes

1 ounce vodka

1 ounce peach schnapps

1 ounce orange juice

4 to 6 ounces lemon-lime soda

1. Fill a shaker with ice and pour in the vodka, peach schnapps, and orange juice. Shake until the shaker is frosty.

2. Strain into a tall glass filled with ice. Fill the rest of the glass with lemon-lime soda.

NOTE: This recipe is gluten free if using a gluten-free vodka.

YIELD: 12 STRAWBERRIES
PREP TIME: 1 HOUR
TO OVERNIGHT
COOK TIME: 2 MINUTES
V, V+, GF

"Bring Out the Flavor" Champagne Strawberries

Inspired by: *Pretty Woman*

When Edward Lewis invites Vivian Ward, a sex worker with a heart of gold, up to his room, he schmoozes her with a bottle of bubbly and a bowl of ripe strawberries to bring out the flavor of the Champagne. In this recipe, the Champagne brings out the flavor of the strawberries. Covered in chocolate and arranged in the shape of Vivian's ruby necklace, this sweet treat is a sure thing. Skipping over this one would be a big mistake. HUGE.

12 strawberries, with stems attached

375 milliliters Champagne (or sparkling white wine)

10 ounces white chocolate candy melts

1 tablespoon coconut oil

1. Wash the strawberries and place into a large bowl.

2. Pour the Champagne into the bowl, covering the strawberries. Cover with a lid or plastic wrap and let soak overnight. (The strawberries can soak for a minimum of one hour, but the longer you soak, the boozier the strawberries will be!)

3. Line a plate with paper towels. Gently strain the strawberry-Champagne mixture, discarding the liquid. Pat the strawberries dry with a paper towel and place them on the paper towel–lined plate.

4. In a double boiler, melt the candy melts and coconut oil, mixing together. (No double boiler? Place the candy melts and coconut oil in a microwave-safe bowl and heat for 30 seconds at a time, stirring in between.)

5. Dip the strawberries in the melted candy mixture and lay flat on wax paper to harden.

6. Arrange in the shape of a necklace and serve.

THE COLONIAL WOMAN

Inspired by: *Bridesmaids*

YIELD: 1 DRINK
PREP TIME: 5 MINUTES
V, V+, GF*

Life is full of trials and tribulations, like dealing with nosy roommates and trying to keep your lunch down after eating some bad meat. But nothing is harder than serving as your best friend's bridesmaid when your own love life is in shambles. If you're struggling to get through your bestie's bachelorette weekend before the plane has even taken off, a stiff drink might help take the edge off. All the ingredients for this cocktail can be found in the average flight attendant's drink cart. Warning: If you see a colonial woman churning butter on the wing of the plane, it's time to switch to water. And, please, stay in your assigned seat.

2 mini bottles (or 3.4 ounces) Scotch

6 ounces ginger ale

1 lemon wedge

1. Ask for two mini bottles of Scotch, ginger ale, a lemon wedge, a stirrer stick, and a cup of ice while on a plane.

2. Pour the bottles of Scotch into the cup of ice, and then squeeze the lemon wedge over.

3. Top with ginger ale and lightly stir together.

4. Sip, relax, and ignore the colonial woman on the wing.

NOTE: This recipe is gluten free if using a gluten-free Scotch.

YIELD: 1 DRINK
PREP TIME: 2 MINUTES
V, V+ GF*

You've Got Cocktail: New York in the Fall

Inspired by: *You've Got Mail*

Don't you love New York in the fall? The air is crisp, the trees are golden, and the smell of love is in the air . . . or is that fresh school supplies? The cozy vibe makes it easy to fall in love with anyone, like the anonymous pen pal you've been emailing back and forth with or the rich guy who shut down your beautiful little bookshop—hey, why not both? Book lovers of all sizes, types, and corporate structures will enjoy this drink inspired by the season: It's like a Manhattan with hints of apple cider and cinnamon. It'll bring to mind warm cardigans and leaves crunching under your feet, with just a hint of scotch tape.

Ice

2 ounces rye whiskey

1 ounce cold apple cider

2 dashes angostura bitters

1 dash ground cinnamon

1 maraschino cherry

1. Place the ice along with the whiskey, apple cider, bitters, and cinnamon in a cocktail shaker, and shake until the shaker is frosted.

2. Strain the drink into a coupe glass and garnish with a maraschino cherry.

NOTE: This recipe is gluten free if using gluten-free rye whiskey.

Thirteen Going on Thirty, Flirty and Thriving Daiquiri

Inspired by: *13 Going on 30*

After making a birthday wish to be thirty, flirty, and thriving, thirteen-year-old Jenna Rink wakes up one day to find herself a thirty-year-old magazine editor that works (kind of) hard and plays even harder. She's excited to finally partake in grown-up beverages but still has the taste of a kid. Though many of her peers have moved on to wine, she's ordering frozen, fruity, hangovers-in-a-cup. This daiquiri is Jenna Rink in a glass: sweet, frothy, and rimmed with a magic wishing dust of nostalgic candy. Drink while listening to "Love Is a Battlefield."

DAIQUIRI:

½ cup frozen strawberries

2 ounces light rum

1 ounce freshly squeezed lime juice

1 ounce simple syrup

GARNISHES (OPTIONAL):

Popping candy

2 lime wedges

Candy necklace

1 strawberry

Gummy bear candies

SPECIAL TOOL:

Cocktail pick

TO MAKE THE DAIQUIRI:

1. Blend the frozen strawberries, rum, lime juice, and simple syrup in a blender until smooth.

TO GARNISH:

2. Pour the popping candy on a small plate. Slide a lime wedge around the rim of a stemmed cocktail glass, then dip the rim into the popping candy until covered. Wrap a candy necklace around the base of the glass.

3. Fill the glass with the daiquiri and top with the remaining lime wedge, a strawberry, and gummy bear candies skewered onto a cocktail pick.

NOTES: Thirteen and not quite thirty? This drink is just as tasty without the rum—just substitute 2 ounces of water.

This recipe is gluten free, vegetarian, and vegan if using gluten-free, vegan gummy bears.

POISONOUS APPLE MARTINI: ONE SIP IS ALL IT TAKES

Inspired by: *Enchanted*

Once upon a time, an animated wicked queen pushed animated princess Giselle down a well, where she was transported to modern-day New York City. And even though every fairy-tale character should know to avoid questionable-looking apples, Giselle couldn't resist a complimentary apple martini. You can make your own version below, but be careful—they're "poison"! The only remedy is true love's first kiss, so share this drink with a handsome prince if you want to live happily ever after.

½ cup ice

2 ounces vodka

2 ounces sour apple liquor

3 ounces cranberry juice cocktail

1 very thin apple slice

1. Chill a martini glass in the freezer.

2. Place the ice, vodka, sour apple liquor, and cranberry juice in a cocktail shaker and shake until the shaker is frosted.

3. Strain the mixture into the chilled martini glass and garnish with the apple slice.

NOTE: This recipe is gluten free if using a gluten-free vodka.

YIELD: 1 DRINK
PREP TIME: 20 MINUTES
V, V+, GF

YOUR GLASS OR MINE: GARDEN GLORY

Inspired by: *Your Place or Mine*

When you're not sure if you're in the mood for a cocktail or a crudité, the Garden Glory is always a safe choice. Debbie Dunn and her best friend, Peter Coleman, live on separate coasts, which might as well be separate worlds, so Debbie doesn't know what she's getting into when she orders this elaborate drink at a New York City bar. Is it a drink? Is it food? So many questions, and they just keep coming. Is it friendship? Is it love? You might need to mix another round while you mull this one over.

TOMATO ROSE:

1 Roma tomato

VEGETABLE SKEWER:

2 cucumbers, divided

1 pickled carrot, cut into ½-inch squares

1 radish

COCKTAIL:

Juice of 1 lime

¼ cup fresh spinach

1 jalapeño slice, sliced in half crosswise

2 ounces tequila

½ ounce simple syrup

Ice

2 ounces sparkling water

GARNISHES:

6 cherry tomatoes

1 pickled asparagus spear

1 petite carrot, sliced in half vertically

1 lime wheel

1 sprig rosemary

SPECIAL TOOL:

6-inch skewer

TO MAKE THE TOMATO ROSE:

1. Cut a thin slice from the base of the tomato, stopping about three-quarters of the way through the slice. From there, start cutting a ¾-inch-thick slice of mostly skin, rotating up the tomato to create a thin ribbon. Continue turning the tomato while peeling the skin until you get to the top. Roll the tomato ribbon up into a rose shape, tucking the base onto the bottom of the flower. Set aside.

TO MAKE THE VEGETABLE SKEWER:

2. Using a vegetable peeler, peel a long ribbon from one cucumber. Place the cucumber ribbon halfway down the skewer, then add a carrot square. Wrap the cucumber ribbon over the carrot and pierce through the top of the skewer again. Continue adding carrots and wrapping the cucumber, alternating sides of the cucumber until it's used up. Cut the radish in half vertically and place one half on the top of the skewer. Set aside.

TO MAKE THE COCKTAIL:

3. Finish peeling the cucumber and place it with the lime juice, spinach, and jalapeño slice in a blender. Blend until smooth but pulpy. Strain and keep the juice, discarding the solids.

4. Place the blended juice, tequila, and simple syrup in a cocktail shaker filled with ice and shake until the shaker is frosted. Cut the remaining cucumber into thin rounds and line a large goblet with the rounds.

TO GARNISH:

5. Fill one-quarter of the goblet with ice. Pour in the drink from the cocktail shaker and the sparkling water, then top with the cherry tomatoes. Garnish with the tomato rose, vegetable skewer, pickled asparagus, petite carrot, lime wheel, and rosemary sprig.

chapter
three

THE MORNING AFTER

Rise and shine! It's morning, and whether you're waking up alone
or sneaking stealthily out of the bedroom after going home with a
cutie from the bar last night, a large breakfast will help start your
day right. Try an elegant Breakfast at Tiffany's if you're feeling
bright-eyed and bushy-tailed, or throw together some beignets if
you're fighting a hangover. Bonus points if you're sharing the meal
with that anonymous bar cutie!

ROMAN HOLIDAY CAFFÈ: THE SHAKERATO

Inspired by: *Roman Holiday*

When in Rome, eat as the Romans eat. But even if you can't hop on a Vespa and take a full culinary tour of the Italian city, you can still enjoy a Shakerato just like the one Joe Bradley orders when he and Princess Ann sit down for an afternoon drink. This recipe is fit for royalty, making a lightly sweetened, foamy iced coffee that's perfect for sipping at an outdoor café.

Ice

2 ounces espresso

1 tablespoon granulated sugar

1. Fill a cocktail shaker with ice.

2. Pour the espresso and sugar into the shaker, and then seal the top.

3. Shake until the shaker is frosted and the beverage is foamy, about 20 seconds.

4. Strain the drink into a coupe glass and serve.

BREAKFAST AT TIFFANY'S

YIELD: 16 CROISSANTS
PREP TIME: 20 MINUTES
COOK TIME: 15 MINUTES
V

Inspired by: *Breakfast at Tiffany's*

It's the most iconic breakfast of all time: Just after dawn on a quiet New York City sidewalk, Holly Golightly exits a taxi and eats her paper-bag breakfast of croissant and coffee while perusing the windows of Tiffany & Co., dreaming of life on the other side of the glass. Who but Holly could look so glamorous eating a flaky, buttery croissant? If your spontaneous, carefree lifestyle doesn't allow you the time to make croissants from scratch, you can create Holly's humble breakfast in thirty minutes with this recipe using premade puff pastry dough. These rich pastries have a Tiffany-worthy blue center and diamond-like sparkling sugar. Share them if you'd like, but it's okay if you want them to belong only to you.

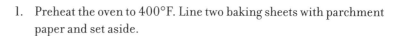

1 cup cream cheese

1 to 2 drops teal food coloring

1 sheet frozen puff pastry dough, thawed

Flour, for the work surface

1 egg

1 tablespoon water

2 tablespoons sparkling sugar

1. Preheat the oven to 400°F. Line two baking sheets with parchment paper and set aside.

2. In a medium bowl, add the cream cheese and mix in the teal food coloring until the color matches Tiffany's signature blue. Set aside.

3. Place the thawed puff pastry dough on a floured surface and roll it out slightly thinner. The dough should grow about 1 inch longer on each side, still forming a square.

4. In order to make 16 tall triangles, begin by cutting the pastry dough in half, and then cut each half into 4 equal rectangles. Cut those rectangles diagonally to make the tall triangles.

5. Place 1 teaspoon of the teal cream cheese at the widest part (the bottom) of each triangle and spread it about halfway up the length of the triangle.

6. Starting at the bottom (widest) part of the triangle, roll the pastry up the entire length. Turn the edges of the rolled pastry towards each other, making a croissant shape. Place the croissant on the prepared baking sheets and repeat with the remaining triangles.

7. In a small bowl, beat the egg with the water and brush the egg wash on the top of each croissant. Sprinkle with sparkling sugar.

8. Bake for 12 to 15 minutes or until golden brown.

9. Serve from a bag with a cup of coffee and head outside to visit your favorite window display.

Date #50 Waffles

Inspired by: *50 First Dates*

You only get one chance to make a first impression—unless the object of your affection has been diagnosed with anterograde amnesia. When Henry Roth discovers Lucy Whitmore constructing a house out of waffles at the Hukilau Cafe, he initially rebuffs her but soon finds that her memory effectively resets every morning, giving him plenty of chances to say "aloha." Construct your own waffle house with this Hawaiian-inspired recipe full of fresh island flavors like coconut and macadamia nuts. It's a scrumptious breakfast to top off a first—or fiftieth—date.

YIELD: 8 WAFFLES
PREP TIME: 15 MINUTES
COOK TIME: 10 MINUTES
V

2 cups all-purpose flour

1 tablespoon baking powder

2 tablespoons granulated sugar

½ teaspoon kosher salt

2 large eggs, separated into yolks and whites

1⅔ cups whole milk

⅓ cup butter, melted

1 teaspoon vanilla extract

½ cup sweetened shredded coconut

½ cup macadamia nuts, finely chopped

Nonstick cooking spray, for greasing

SPECIAL TOOL:
Toothpicks

1. Preheat a square waffle maker to 400°F.

2. In a large bowl, mix together the flour, baking powder, sugar, and salt. Set aside.

3. In a smaller bowl, mix together the egg yolks, milk, butter, and vanilla.

4. Place the egg whites in the bowl of a stand mixer (or in a medium mixing bowl if using a hand mixer) and mix on medium-high speed until stiff peaks form, about 5 minutes.

5. Pour the egg yolk mixture into the flour mixture and mix together. Using a silicone spatula, fold in the coconut and macadamia nuts, and then fold in the egg whites.

6. Spray the waffle maker with nonstick cooking spray, then place ¼ cup of batter into each quarter of the maker (see note). Cook for 3 to 5 minutes or until golden brown. Repeat with the rest of the batter.

7. Separate the waffle squares and prepare them by cutting out windows and areas for doors with a small paring knife, keeping the remnants to be used as doors and other decor. Build the base of a house by standing up four squares and using them to create the walls of a house. Top with another waffle for the roof. Get creative with it! If the waffles won't stay up on their own, try using a toothpick. (They make great hinges for doors!)

NOTE: Waffle makers differ slightly. Please defer to the batter quantities suggested by your maker.

RULE #23 SCONES

Inspired by: *Wedding Crashers*

Rule number one of wedding crashing: Never leave a fellow crasher behind—no matter how traumatic a night you may have had. Jeremy Grey may want to flee the Cleary's compound after his unexpected night of horrors, but as a true wingman, he stays the course. Until John Beckwith has sealed the deal with his wedding date, Jeremy might as well sit back and relax with some of these delicious, summery, lemon-blueberry scones. Don't forget rule number twenty-three: There's nothing wrong with having seconds.

2 cups all-purpose flour

⅓ cup granulated sugar

1 tablespoon lemon zest (from 1 lemon)

1½ teaspoons baking powder

½ teaspoon kosher salt

½ cup unsalted butter, cold and cut into cubes

½ cup heavy cream (can also use heavy whipping cream)

1 cup blueberries, fresh or frozen (do not thaw, if frozen)

1 egg

½ tablespoon turbinado sugar

Butter, for serving

1. Preheat the oven to 375°F and line a baking sheet with parchment paper. Set aside.

2. In a large bowl, mix together the flour, sugar, lemon zest, baking powder, and salt, and then cut in the butter with a pastry cutter or your hands. Combine until everything is fully mixed and slightly crumbly. Slowly add the cream and mix with a hand mixer or wooden spoon until it begins to form a solid dough. Mix in the blueberries.

3. Divide the dough in two and form each half into a disc about 1½ inches thick.

4. Cut each disk into six equal triangles (similar to how you would cut a pizza) and place the triangles on the baking sheet, leaving ½ inch between each one.

5. Beat the egg in a small bowl and brush the top of each triangle. Sprinkle each triangle with turbinado sugar.

6. Bake for 14 to 18 minutes or until fully set in the centers and lightly golden.

7. Serve warm with butter.

BEIGNETS AND THE JETS

Inspired by: *27 Dresses*

When you're always the bridesmaid and never the bride, you might start to give up on finding a love of your own. Maybe it's time to let your guard down a little bit. Do a few shots, turn on your electric boobs, wear your mohair suit, and make some walrus sounds with that person you've been pushing away. It's easy to open up after spending a night dancing on the bar together. The next day, you'll need to recover from that wild night out with something fried, glutenous, and sweet. Something like b-b-b-beignets (and the jets). These delicious treats will make up for any morning-after regrets you may have.

1½ teaspoons active dry yeast

¾ cups warm water

¼ cup granulated sugar, divided

½ teaspoon kosher salt

1 egg

½ cup evaporated milk

3½ cups all-purpose flour, plus more for the work surface

2 tablespoons shortening

4 cups canola oil, plus more for greasing

1 cup powdered sugar

SPECIAL TOOL:
Kitchen thermometer

1. Place the yeast, warm water, and 1 teaspoon of sugar in the bowl of a stand mixer with a dough hook attachment (or a large mixing bowl if using a hand mixer). Lightly mix on low speed just for a moment and let sit for 5 minutes, until foamy.

2. Add the rest of the sugar, the salt, egg, and evaporated milk to the mixing bowl. Mix together.

3. Mix in 1 cup of flour and the shortening. Continue to add the rest of the flour, ½ cup at a time, while mixing on low speed. Increase the speed to medium and continue to mix until the contents have fully incorporated into a dough.

4. Place the dough in an oiled bowl and cover the bowl with plastic wrap. Let rise for at least 2 hours (but it can be left overnight).

5. Line a cooling rack with paper towels and set aside. Take the dough out of the bowl and place it on a floured surface. Roll it into a rectangle about ⅛-inch thick, and then cut the dough in a grid pattern, making 2-inch squares.

6. Pour the canola oil into a deep fryer or Dutch oven, making sure the oil is at least 3 inches deep, and set the fryer to medium heat. While waiting for the oil to heat, pour the powdered sugar in a paper lunch bag or large bowl. Once the oil reaches 350°F, you can begin frying.

7. Place four or five beignets in the fryer (avoid crowding) and cook for about 2 minutes, flipping them with tongs at least once, until both sides are golden brown.

8. Remove the beignets and move them to the prepared cooling rack for 30 seconds before tossing them in the powdered sugar.

9. Repeat steps 7 and 8 with the rest of the beignets.

THE PROPROLLSAL: LIVING IN SIN-NAMON ROLLS

Inspired by: *The Proposal*

YIELD: 12
CINNAMON ROLLS
PREP TIME: 2 HOURS
COOK TIME: 25 MINUTES
V

Waking up with your fiancé to breakfast in bed made by his family sounds like a dream come true—but unfortunately for Margaret Tate, it's a sticky situation. Her green-card engagement to her assistant Andrew Paxton starts to feel more and more real as she realizes what it's like to have a loving family. Show your own family, friends, or even just yourself some love with these delicious cinnamon rolls, covered with caramel sauce and pecans.

DOUGH:

¾ cup whole milk

¼ cup granulated sugar

2¼ teaspoons (1 packet) active dry yeast

¼ cup unsalted butter, melted and slightly cooled

1 egg, room temperature

4 cups flour, plus more for the work surface

1 teaspoon baking powder

½ teaspoon salt

FILLING:

⅓ cup unsalted butter, softened

¾ cup brown sugar

1 tablespoon ground cinnamon

CARAMEL SAUCE:

1 cup granulated sugar

¼ cup unsalted butter, cubed

½ cup heavy cream, room temperature (can also use heavy whipping cream)

½ teaspoon vanilla extract

⅛ teaspoon salt

½ cup chopped pecans

TO MAKE THE DOUGH:

1. In a microwave-safe dish, microwave the milk for 30 seconds and place in the bowl of a stand mixer with a dough hook attachment (or a large mixing bowl if using a hand mixer). Stir in the sugar and sprinkle in the active dry yeast. Let sit for 5 minutes.

2. Add the melted butter, then mix in the egg on low speed.

3. In a separate large mixing bowl, combine the flour, baking powder, and salt, and then slowly add it to the milk mixture and mix on low speed just until everything is combined. Increase the mixer speed to medium, letting the dough hook knead the dough for 8 to 10 minutes. Cover the bowl with a kitchen towel and let rise for 1 hour, or until the dough has doubled in size.

TO MAKE THE FILLING:

4. Line a 9-by-13-inch baking pan with parchment paper and set aside. Take the dough out and roll it into a 14-by-16-inch rectangle on a floured surface. Grease the pan with the butter.

5. In a small bowl, mix together the brown sugar and cinnamon and then sprinkle evenly all over the surface of the dough. Gently press it in until everything is covered.

6. Starting on one of the long sides, tightly roll the dough into a log and let it rest with the end seam on the bottom, helping seal it. Using a serrated knife or a long piece of unflavored dental floss, cut the uneven edges off. Cut the rest of the dough into 12 even rolls about 1⅓ inches thick.

7. Place the rolls into the prepared baking pan (they should be close and touching). Cover the pan with plastic wrap and let rise for 30 minutes.

TO MAKE THE CARAMEL SAUCE:

8. While the dough rises, preheat the oven to 350°F. Place the sugar in a medium saucepan over medium heat and cook, stirring constantly, until the sugar liquifies and becomes brown, 5 to 6 minutes. Add the butter and then the cream, whisking constantly. Let the mixture boil for 1 minute, then remove from the heat. Stir in the vanilla, salt, and pecans and set aside.

9. Remove the plastic wrap from the dough and bake the cinnamon rolls for 20 to 25 minutes or until slightly browned.

10. Once the rolls are out of the oven, let cool for 5 minutes and then spoon the caramel sauce on top. Serve in bed.

Forever February Breakfast Cake

Inspired by: *Groundhog Day*

YIELD: 1 CAKE
PREP TIME: 1 HOUR 20 MINUTES
COOK TIME: 40 MINUTES
V

After repeating the same day over and over, weatherman Phil Connors has learned there's nothing he can do that won't be reset by morning.

. . . nothing he can do that won't be reset by morning.

. . . nothing he can do that won't be reset by—well, you get the idea. When Phil's forecast predicts nothing but February 2nd for the foreseeable future, he decides to have some fun with his time loop and eat whatever he wants for breakfast. He indulges in some angel food cake with strawberry whipped cream frosting, leaving his breakfast date a little disgusted but also intrigued. Next time you're stuck in a rut, make this breakfast cake to bring some joy and spontaneity to your morning.

CAKE:

1½ cups granulated sugar

1 cup cake flour

¼ teaspoon kosher salt

1½ cups egg whites (from 10 to 12 eggs)

1½ teaspoons cream of tartar

1 teaspoon vanilla extract

Ingredients continued on page 60

TO MAKE THE CAKE:

1. Preheat the oven to 350°F.

2. Place the granulated sugar in a food processor and pulse until sugar is a fine texture.

3. In a small bowl, mix together ¾ cup of the processed sugar, the cake flour, and salt. Set aside.

4. Place the egg whites in the bowl of a stand mixer fitted with a whisk attachment (or a large mixing bowl if using a hand mixer) and whisk on low until the egg whites are frothy, about 1 minute. Add in the cream of tartar.

5. Increase the mixer to medium speed, and slowly add the remaining ¾ cup of sugar while mixing, 1 tablespoon at a time. (As you add the sugar, tablespoon after tablespoon, again, then again, you may find yourself thinking like Phil, contemplating what matters most in this life.)

6. Increase the mixer to medium-high speed and mix until soft peaks begin to form, 5 to 6 minutes.

7. Remove the bowl from the mixer. Fold in the vanilla, and then fold in the flour mixture ¼ cup at a time. Gently mix with a silicone spatula until fully incorporated.

8. Spoon the batter into an ungreased tube pan. Give a quick swirl through the batter with a knife to break up any air bubbles and smooth the top.

FROSTING:

1 cup strawberries

1 cup whipping cream

½ teaspoon vanilla extract

½ cup powdered sugar

SPECIAL TOOL:

Tube pan

9. Bake for 35 to 40 minutes, or until the cake bounces back from a gentle push and a toothpick inserted in the middle comes out clean.

10. Cool upside down in the pan for 1 hour. While the cake is cooling, make the frosting.

TO MAKE THE FROSTING:

11. Chill the bowl of a stand mixer (or a large mixing bowl if using a hand mixer). Purée the strawberries in a blender until smooth, and then strain through a fine-mesh sieve, discarding the liquid. Place the purée in a medium bowl and set aside.

12. Whisk the whipping cream on high speed in the chilled mixer bowl until soft peaks begin to form, about 6 minutes. Add the vanilla, powdered sugar, and strawberry purée and whisk on high for another 2 to 3 minutes or until stiff peaks form.

13. Scrape a butter knife along the edge of the tube pan and invert onto a serving plate to release the cake.

14. Use a silicone spatula to cover the top and side of the cake with the frosting.

BREAKFAST OF CHAMPIONS

Inspired by: *Forgetting Sarah Marshall*

It's not easy to forget an ex after a break-up. Everything reminds you of them, from your favorite breakfast diner to that rock opera song you heard one time when you were in the car together. Sometimes the only way to escape is to hop on a plane and fly to a luxurious island resort—except in Peter Bretter's case he comes face-to-face with his ex, Sarah Marshall, and her new rock-star boyfriend. Bummer. Luckily, the resort staff takes pity on him and slips him some perks, including a bonus bottle of coconut rum for his cocktail. This breakfast of champions isn't your average morning power smoothie, but it's a nice vacation treat. (Not relaxing at a resort? Omit the rum for a perfectly delicious tropical mocktail.)

3.4 ounces (or 2 mini bottles) coconut rum

6 ounces passion fruit–orange-guava juice

1 banana

½ cup ice

1. Place the rum, juice, banana, and ice in a blender.

2. Blend until smooth (about 30 seconds).

3. Pour into a daiquiri glass.

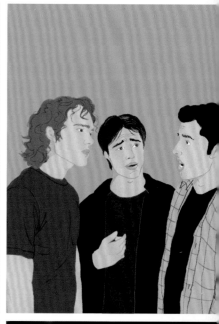

chapter
four

LONG-TERM RELATIONSHIP

You're past those initial butterflies of a new romance and have
moved onto the easy comfort of a long-term relationship. This is
the main course of your love life. It's substantial! It nourishes you!
And it's delicious, just like the food in this chapter. These recipes
are great for a cozy night at home for two but nice enough to serve
when hosting your future in-laws for the first time. What, you
didn't think you could avoid that agonizing milestone, did you?

It's (Not Too) Complicated Croque Monsieur

Inspired by: *It's Complicated*

Love, marriage, divorce, breakups, makeups, and unexpectedly NSFW video calls can all be very, very complicated. You know what's not complicated? A Croque Monsieur. Whether you're young and broke in Paris or sharing an evening with your new crush a couple of wrinkles down the road, a Croque Monsieur is an easy yet delicious meal. Though it comes together quickly and is made with simple, inexpensive ingredients, it's a sandwich that's truly greater than the sum of its parts.

BÉCHAMEL SAUCE:

1 tablespoon salted butter

1 tablespoon all-purpose flour

⅓ cup whole milk

Dash ground mustard

Dash ground nutmeg

Dashes salt and pepper

SANDWICHES:

2 tablespoons salted butter

4 slices crusty French bread

2 teaspoons Dijon mustard

1 cup shredded Gruyère cheese, divided

4 thin slices deli ham

Dash cayenne pepper

TO MAKE THE BÉCHAMEL SAUCE:

1. Melt the butter in a medium saucepan over medium heat. Whisk in the flour and cook, stirring constantly, for 90 seconds or until the flour is a light brown color. Slowly add the milk, whisking constantly, and then continue to whisk until the sauce is thickened, about 3 minutes. Remove from the heat and mix in the ground mustard, nutmeg, and salt and pepper. Set aside.

TO MAKE THE SANDWICHES:

2. Set the oven to broil and heat a large skillet on the stove over medium-high heat.

3. Spread about 1 teaspoon of butter on one side of each bread slice. Place the bread butter side down on the skillet and spread béchamel sauce on two of the slices and Dijon mustard on the other two. Sprinkle ¼ cup of Gruyère over the béchamel sauce–coated slices, then place two slices of ham on top of the cheese. Top with the Dijon-coated slice, butter side up.

4. Cook the sandwiches for 2 minutes on each side, or until the bread is golden brown and has a light crunch.

5. Place the sandwiches on a cookie sheet and sprinkle the tops with the rest of the shredded Gruyère, followed by a dash of cayenne.

6. Broil sandwiches for 90 seconds or until cheese is melted. Serve.

10 Things I Hate Pad See Ew

Inspired by: *10 Things I Hate About You*

Ten things you'll love about this Thai dish:

    1) It will win over a "dangerous" woman (or any person).

    2) It pairs perfectly with feminist prose and angry girl rock music of the indie persuasion.

    3) It's a great treat after a game of paintball or a night at Club Skunk.

    4) Okay, we didn't get to 10 . . . not even close, not even a little bit, not even at all.

2 tablespoons soy sauce

2 teaspoons black soy sauce

1 tablespoon oyster sauce

2 teaspoons granulated sugar

2½ tablespoons vegetable oil, divided

1 large chicken breast

3 cloves garlic, minced

2 cups Chinese broccoli (or broccolini), leaves and stems separated and cut diagonally into 2-inch pieces

2 eggs

1 pound fresh wide rice noodles (or 8 ounces dried wide rice noodles, cooked according to the package directions)

1. In a small bowl, mix the soy sauce, black soy sauce, oyster sauce, and sugar together. Set aside.

2. In a wok or large frying pan over medium-high heat, heat 1 tablespoon of vegetable oil. Slice the chicken into thin, bite-size pieces and then add it to the hot wok. Cook the chicken for 2 minutes on one side, then flip and cook for another 1 to 2 minutes, until the chicken is firm with no more pink. Set the chicken aside.

3. Add 1 tablespoon of oil, the garlic, and the broccoli stems to the wok. Cook, stirring constantly, for 2 minutes and then add the broccoli leaves. Gently mix everything together while cooking for another 30 seconds.

4. Push the ingredients of the wok to one side and add the remaining ½ tablespoon of oil and the eggs to the empty side. Scramble, then cut the eggs with a spatula and mix into the rest of the stir-fry. Remove the contents of the wok into a large bowl and set aside.

5. Place the noodles and sauce mixture into the wok and cook, moving the noodles occasionally, 1 to 2 minutes or until the noodles have caramelized. Add the chicken and the garlic-broccoli-egg mixture back into the wok and cook for another 30 seconds, or until everything is combined and covered in sauce.

6. Separate into two bowls and enjoy.

Eat, Pray, and Eat Some More

Inspired by: *Eat Pray Love*

"You American girls, when you come to Italy, all you want is pasta and sausage." Liz Gilbert didn't opt for the sausage during the Italian leg of her transformative transcontinental trip, but everyone's journey of self-discovery is different, so don't shy away if the sausage is calling to you. For seekers of inner happiness and balanced flavor, this handmade pasta recipe is for you. You'll feel like you're dining in Italy, no plane ticket needed.

SPAGHETTI:

¼ teaspoon kosher salt

2 cups all-purpose flour

3 eggs

1 teaspoon olive oil

SAUCE:

½ tablespoon olive oil

2 cloves garlic, minced

28-ounce can San Marzano
    peeled tomatoes

¼ teaspoon kosher salt

¼ teaspoon freshly ground black pepper

Pinch red pepper flakes

2 tablespoons chopped fresh basil

SAUSAGE:

1 tablespoon olive oil

2 Italian sausage links

GARNISH:

2 tablespoons pecorino cheese, grated

SPECIAL TOOL:

Kitchen thermometer

TO MAKE THE SPAGHETTI:

1. In a small bowl, mix the salt into the flour and then pour the mixture into a mound on a clean surface. Make a well in the flour and add the eggs and olive oil. Carefully beat the eggs and oil together with a fork, and then start to incorporate the flour until a dough begins to form. Sprinkle more flour around the dough, then knead the dough for 5 minutes or until it's smooth and elastic. Cover with a towel and let rest for 30 minutes.

2. Cover a baking sheet or wire cooling rack with a towel and set aside. Roll the dough into a thin sheet, about ¹⁄₁₆-inch thick. Place the dough through a pasta maker or cut long thin strips about ¼ inch wide. Place the noodles on the prepared baking sheet or cooling rack to dry for 30 minutes.

TO MAKE THE SAUCE:

3. In a large sauce pot over medium heat, heat the olive oil and add the minced garlic, sautéing for 30 seconds. Add the tomatoes, salt, black pepper, and red pepper flakes and lightly break up the tomatoes with a potato masher or wooden spoon. Bring to a simmer for 10 minutes or until the sauce has reduced slightly. Add the basil and simmer for another 20 minutes or until the sauce has thickened.

TO COOK THE SAUSAGE:

4. In a large frying pan or grill pan, heat the olive oil over medium-high heat and then add the sausage links. Cook for 6 to 8 minutes, then flip over. Cook for another 6 minutes or until sausages are slightly charred and reach an internal temperature of 160°F.

5. Cook the dried noodles in a large pot of boiling salted water for 2 to 3 minutes or until al dente.

6. Place 1 cup of pasta on a plate and top with ½ cup of sauce. Place a sausage on the side and top the entire plate with a sprinkling of pecorino cheese. *Buon appetito!*

CRAZY RICH DUMPLINGS

Inspired by: *Crazy Rich Asians*

Joining family traditions is a great way to get to know your future in-laws, and for the Young family, that tradition is making dumplings. Whether your method of dumpling folding is to "put the baby in bed" or "put the Botox in the face," you will make memories (and a delicious meal). Invite your friends and family to help you and turn the meal prep into a fun activity! No guilt trip needed.

WRAPPER:

4 cups all-purpose flour

1½ cups room-temperature water

1 tablespoon vegetable oil

1 pinch salt

FILLING:

1 pound ground pork

½ cup minced green onions
(about 6 green onions)

1 egg

2 tablespoons minced garlic
(about 6 cloves garlic)

2 tablespoons minced ginger
(about 2 inches ginger)

1 tablespoon sesame oil

2 tablespoons soy sauce

2 tablespoons Shaoxing wine

1 teaspoon salt

¼ teaspoon white pepper

1 tablespoon canola oil

DUMPLING SAUCE:

1½ inch ginger knob, peeled and minced

1 tablespoon black vinegar

1 teaspoon soy sauce

Dash chile oil

SPECIAL TOOL:

Steamer tray

TO MAKE THE WRAPPER:

1. In a large bowl, combine the flour, water, vegetable oil, and salt. Mix and knead in the bowl for 10 minutes or until it creates a soft, firm, stretchy dough. Cover the bowl with plastic wrap and let rest for 30 minutes.

TO MAKE THE FILLING:

2. In a large bowl, mix the ground pork, green onions, egg, garlic, ginger, sesame oil, soy sauce, Shaoxing wine, salt, and white pepper, cover with plastic wrap, and refrigerate until needed.

3. Take the dough and roll it into a long log, about 1 inch in diameter. Cut the dough into about fifty 1-inch balls and place on a large plate or work surface. Work with a few pieces of dough at a time, keeping the rest covered in plastic wrap.

4. Using your palm, flatten the balls into disks, and then use a rolling pin to roll the disks into thin circles 3 inches in diameter. The edges should be thinner than the middle. Set aside and continue rolling until all the dough balls have been flattened.

5. Remove the filling from the refrigerator. Roll 1 tablespoon of filling between two spoons, making a football shape with the filling, and set it aside on a large plate or baking sheet. Repeat with the rest of the filling.

6. Take a wrapper and place a filling ball in the center of the bottom half of the wrapper. Wet your fingers in a small bowl of water, and then wet the top edge of the wrapper. Fold the wrapper up and crease it three times on each side, then give it a final pinch in the middle to ensure it is closed. Place it on a steamer tray.

7. Repeat steps 4 through 6 to make the rest of the dumplings.

8. Place the dumplings in a steamer, being careful not to overcrowd, and steam for 10 minutes or until fully cooked through. (To test, take one

out and cut it open to confirm the meat is fully cooked.) If you don't have a steamer, heat 2 tablespoons of oil in a large pan over medium-high heat. Place the dumplings in the pan and cover the bottom of the pan in a small layer of water. Cover, reduce the heat to medium, and let cook for 10 minutes or until fully cooked through.

9. Heat 1 tablespoon of canola oil in a large frying pan, and gently fry the cooked dumplings for 2 minutes.

10. Continue steaming and frying the rest of the dumplings.

TO MAKE THE DUMPLING SAUCE:

11. Place the minced ginger in a small bowl and cover it with the black vinegar, soy sauce, and chile oil. Give a light mix and dip your dumplings!

She's Ball That: Supersized Falafel Balls

Inspired by: *She's All That*

Cue the catchy '90s pop song. When Laney gets made over from mousey nerd into gorgeous It girl, the transformation is jaw-dropping. And to think, all it took was a haircut and contact lenses . . . and it didn't hurt that she ditched the falafel hat from her after-school job. That uniform is definitely not all that, but the menu is quite delicious. Go ahead and supersize your balls for this falafel recipe, and have some tahini or spicy hummus on the side for some added flavor that's, well, not improved but . . . different.

1 cup dried chickpeas

Canola oil, for frying

¾ cup fresh cilantro

¾ cup fresh parsley

½ cup chopped yellow onion (about 1 onion)

3 cloves garlic, peeled

1 tablespoon olive oil

1 teaspoon lemon zest

1 teaspoon cumin

1 teaspoon coriander

¾ teaspoon kosher salt

¼ teaspoon cayenne pepper

¼ teaspoon baking soda

Tahini sauce or spicy hummus, for serving

SPECIAL TOOL:
Kitchen thermometer

1. Place the chickpeas in a container of water, enough to fully cover the chickpeas plus another 2 inches. Let soak for 24 hours at room temperature. After soaking, drain and rinse the chickpeas, and then lay them on a paper towel–lined plate. Pat dry.

2. Line a plate with paper towels and set aside. Fill a deep fryer or large heavy pot 3-inches deep with canola oil. Heat over medium heat until the oil reaches 350°F.

3. While the oil heats, place the chickpeas, cilantro, parsley, onion, garlic, olive oil, lemon zest, cumin, coriander, salt, cayenne pepper, and baking soda into a large food processor. Pulse until the mixture is well combined with a cornmeal-like consistency, about 2 minutes, stopping halfway to scrape down the sides with a silicone spatula.

4. Scoop up ¼ cup falafel mix and form into a ball (the balls will be fragile, so handle carefully). Set aside on a large plate and continue with the rest of the mix.

5. Drop the falafel balls into the hot oil, cooking for 3 to 4 minutes or until brown on the outside (the falafel will be green on the inside).

6. Use a skimmer to remove the falafel balls and place on the paper towel–lined plate.

7. Serve drizzled with tahini sauce or dipped in spicy hummus.

Egg Salad Obsession

Inspired by: *The 40-Year-Old Virgin*

YIELD: 2 SANDWICHES
PREP TIME: 20 MINUTES
COOK TIME: 12 MINUTES
V

Hoping to plan an exciting Friday evening for you and your date? How about giving Andy Stitzer's egg salad sandwich a try? This sandwich has all the right flavors, with mayonnaise, onions, and paprika, of course. But, unlike Andy, you won't need to spend three hours on this recipe. Simply mix the ingredients together until they've reached the consistency of, uh . . . a bag of sand? You know what—just follow the recipe for an egg salad that's so delicious, it'll only last a minute.

6 eggs

2 tablespoons minced green onion (about 1 green onion)

¼ cup mayonnaise

¾ teaspoon yellow mustard

¼ teaspoon paprika

¼ teaspoon salt

¼ teaspoon freshly ground black pepper

2 leaves lettuce

4 slices white bread

1. Gently place the whole eggs in the bottom of a large sauce pot and cover them with cold water. Cover the pot and bring the water to boil over high heat. Turn off the heat and let the eggs stay in the pot, slowly cooking, for 12 minutes. Rinse with cold water and peel the eggs.

2. Place the peeled eggs in a large bowl and mash with a fork.

3. Add the green onion, mayonnaise, mustard, paprika, salt, and pepper to the bowl and mix. Taste-test and add more salt or pepper as needed.

4. Place one leaf of lettuce on a piece of bread, and then add a heaping ½ cup of egg salad. Top with another piece of bread.

5. Repeat with the rest of the bread, lettuce, and egg salad to make another sandwich.

TO ME, YOU ARE
PIE-FECT

chapter
five

THE HOLIDAYS

It can be hard to focus on your love life when you're married to your fast-paced job in the big city, but there's no better time than the holidays to escape to a small snowy town, fall in love with a local, and save Christmas. The town twinkles with lights, the hearths glow with fire, and carolers sing on every street corner. It's giving hot cocoa and marshmallows. It's giving spiced cookies. It's giving powdered sugar floating in the air like a dusting of snow. It's a Christmas dream! If you're unable to leave your job behind for a life selling Christmas trees year-round, cozy up with one of these recipes and escape with a holiday movie for a couple hours instead.

White Christmas Platter: Late-Night Sandwiches with Buttermilk

Inspired by: *White Christmas*

YIELD:
6 HALF-SANDWICHES
PREP TIME: 15 MINUTES

Can't sleep and need a late-night snack? Sounds like you could use a sandwich. Choose one from this festive Vermont smorgasbord: ham and cheese on rye if you want to dream about a cool blond; turkey to dream about a brunette; and liverwurst to dream about, well, liverwurst. Dreaming of a white Christmas? Wash it down with a big glass of buttermilk and take your chances. Now, off to bed to get some rest—tomorrow, you have to put on the best show this little town has ever seen!

HAM AND CHEESE SANDWICH:

1 tablespoon mayonnaise

2 slices rye bread

4 slices thinly sliced deli ham

2 slices Swiss cheese

2 pitted olives, each on its own toothpick

TURKEY SANDWICH:

1 tablespoon cream cheese

2 slices wheat bread

1 tablespoon cranberry sauce

4 slices thinly sliced deli turkey

2 slices Havarti cheese

LIVERWURST SANDWICH:

1 tablespoon mustard

2 slices rye bread

2 slices liverwurst

2 thin slices sweet onion

Make each sandwich per the directions below and place on a large platter. Keep in the refrigerator overnight (but no more than a few days) for when you need a late-night snack.

TO MAKE THE HAM AND CHEESE SANDWICH:

1. Spread the mayonnaise on one slice of bread. Top with the slices of ham and cheese and the other piece of bread. Cut on the diagonal and garnish each piece with an olive on a toothpick.

TO MAKE THE TURKEY SANDWICH:

2. Spread the cream cheese on one slice of bread and cranberry sauce on the other. Top the cream cheese-covered bread with the slices of turkey and cheese and place the cranberry-covered piece of bread on top. Cut in the middle to make two rectangle pieces.

TO MAKE THE LIVERWURST SANDWICH:

3. Spread the mustard on one slice of bread. Top with the slices of liverwurst, the onion slices, and the other piece of bread. Cut on the diagonal.

PIE ACTUALLY

Inspired by: *Love Actually*

Let me say, without hope or agenda—just because it's Christmas (and at Christmas you tell the truth), to me, banoffee pie is perfect. And my wasted heart will love its graham cracker crust filled with bananas, whipped cream, and caramel, until the pan is empty. Happy Christmas!

10 graham cracker sheets (about 5 ounces)

1 tablespoon granulated sugar

½ teaspoon kosher salt

¼ cup unsalted butter, melted then cooled

1 teaspoon vanilla extract

One 14-ounce can dulce de leche

4 bananas, peeled and cut into ¼-inch slices

1½ cups whipping cream

¼ cup powdered sugar

1 teaspoon instant coffee

SPECIAL TOOL:

9-inch tart tin

1. Preheat the oven to 400°F.

2. Place the graham crackers, sugar, and salt in a food processor and process to a fine crumb. Add the butter and vanilla and process until fully mixed.

3. Place the crumb mixture into the tart tin and press along the base and sides until the crumb mixture forms an even crust.

4. Put the tin in the oven and bake the crust for 15 to 18 minutes or until dark golden brown.

5. Scoop the dulce de leche into the piecrust and level with a spoon. Place the banana slices on the top of the dulce de leche.

6. In the bowl of a stand mixer (or a large mixing bowl if using a hand mixer), whip the whipping cream, powdered sugar, and instant coffee together until stiff peaks form, about 3 minutes. Place the whipped cream on top of the pie and chill until ready to serve.

THE SPIRITS OF CHRISTMAS

Inspired by: *The Spirit of Christmas*

YIELD: 1 DRINK (PLUS ENOUGH BATTER FOR 7 MORE DRINKS)
PREP TIME: 10 MINUTES
V, GF

On the twelfth day of Christmas my corporeal ghost boyfriend gave to me . . . When estate attorney Kate goes out to get an inn appraised, she finds the inn is haunted by former rum-runner Daniel, who died a mysterious death in the 1920s but somehow still looks incredible in a suit. If you're throwing a Christmas Eve ball, serve one of these Prohibition-era specialties, a Christmas cocktail made with dark rum and cognac. With this drink in your hand, you'll have everything you need to get into the Christmas spirit: a trimmed tree, strung lights, and a century-old murder-by-bludgeoning to solve.

BATTER:

3 eggs, separated

¼ teaspoon cream of tartar

2 tablespoons salted butter, room temperature

1 cup powdered sugar

½ teaspoon vanilla extract

½ teaspoon ground cinnamon

¼ teaspoon ground cloves

¼ teaspoon ground allspice

DRINK:

1 ounce dark rum

1 ounce cognac

1 cup boiling water

Pinch nutmeg, for garnish

TO MAKE THE BATTER:

1. In a small bowl, whisk the egg whites and the cream of tartar until stiff peaks form, about 5 minutes. In a medium bowl, mix together the yolks and butter and then add the sugar, vanilla, cinnamon, cloves, and allspice. Fold the yolk mixture into the egg whites. Refrigerate until needed.

TO MAKE THE DRINK:

2. Place ¼ cup of the batter in a mug. Add the rum and cognac. Pour in the boiling water and mix together.

3. Top the drink with a sprinkling of nutmeg.

CHEF'S SPECIAL RISOTTO

Inspired by: *Last Holiday*

What would you do if you only had a few weeks left to live? Maybe go on a trip, confess to your crush that you love them, and channel your inner gourmand? Finding herself in that exact situation, Georgia Byrd decides to liquidate her assets and spend her last few weeks treating herself like a queen. That includes one last holiday to the deluxe Grandhotel Pupp, where she dines on a gourmet meal prepared by the famous Chef Didier. Georgia orders one of everything, but if you must choose, treat yourself to this rich, creamy risotto that can turn any kitchen into a Michelin-star restaurant. Add this recipe to your scrapbook and pull it out anytime you want to live your best life.

8 baby beets, peeled and cut in half lengthwise

2 tablespoons olive oil, divided

1 teaspoon kosher salt, divided

¼ teaspoon freshly ground black pepper

4 turnips, peeled and cut into ½ inch wedges

4 petite carrots, peeled and cut in half lengthwise

1 rutabaga, peeled and cut into 8 pieces

3 tablespoons salted butter, divided

½ cup diced onion

2 cups risotto rice (arborio or carnaroli)

½ bottle Barolo wine (or other dry red wine, like a pinot noir)

4 cups beef stock

3 tablespoons grated Parmesan cheese

1 tablespoon white truffle oil

Fresh white truffle (optional)

1. Preheat the oven to 400°F. Line two baking sheets with aluminum foil.

2. Place the beets in a medium bowl and cover with ½ tablespoon of olive oil, ¼ teaspoon of salt, and ⅛ teaspoon of black pepper. Gently mix until evenly coated. Place the turnips, carrots, and rutabaga in a large bowl and cover with 1½ tablespoons of olive oil, ½ teaspoon of salt, and ⅛ teaspoon of black pepper. Gently mix until evenly coated.

3. Pour the oiled vegetables onto one of the prepared baking sheets and the beets on the other. Place the sheets on separate oven racks and bake for 45 minutes or until the vegetables are fork-tender.

4. While the vegetables are roasting, in a large saucepan over medium heat, melt 1 tablespoon of butter. Add the diced onion and sauté, stirring often, for 8 minutes or until softened and translucent. Add the rice and mix until fully coated in the onion mixture. Slowly add the wine, then cook for 5 minutes, uncovered, allowing some of the wine to evaporate.

5. While the wine cooks off, place the beef stock in a small saucepan over medium heat. When the stock has just begun simmering, add it to the rice mixture slowly, one ladle at a time, allowing the liquid to absorb before adding more. Continue to add the stock while stirring until the rice is fully cooked (but not mushy), about 20 minutes.

6. Turn off the heat and mix in the remaining 2 tablespoons of butter, the Parmesan, truffle oil, and remaining one-quarter teaspoon of salt. Cover the risotto and let sit for 5 minutes.

7. Scoop one-quarter of the risotto into a bowl, top with one-quarter of the vegetables, and grate fresh truffle shavings on top of that. Repeat for all four servings.

ROYAL WEDDING SLIDERS

Inspired by: *A Christmas Prince: The Royal Wedding*

YIELD: 12 SLIDERS
PREP TIME: 5 MINUTES
COOK TIME: 15 MINUTES

A wedding represents a beautiful merging of two families. But that merging isn't always seamless, like when a royal prince is marrying the daughter of an NYC diner owner. When Amber Moore starts planning her wedding, making sure her dad is the caterer is at the top of the list. "Painted red" with sauce, these sliders are a delicious combination of a hamburger and meatball sub and would be right at home in a diner booth or a fancy ballroom. Want to lean into the Christmas theme? Make half of them green with pesto.

1 tablespoon salted butter

12 brioche slider buns or rolls, split open

2 pounds 80/20 ground beef

1 teaspoon kosher salt

½ teaspoon freshly ground black pepper

½ teaspoon dried basil

¼ teaspoon garlic powder

1 cup shredded mozzarella

1 cup sauce (see page 69)

1. Preheat a griddle or a cast-iron pan over high heat. Butter the inside of each bun and give them a quick toast on the griddle or pan while it's preheating, about 30 seconds. Set the buns open-faced on a large serving plate.

2. In a large bowl, mix the ground beef, salt, pepper, basil, and garlic powder. Divide the beef mixture into 12 equal pieces, roll into loose balls, and press each down to form a patty.

3. Place a few patties onto the hot griddle or pan, cook for 4 minutes, and then flip them over. Sprinkle a heaping tablespoon of shredded mozzarella on the top of each patty. Cook for another 4 minutes or until browned with crispy edges and melted cheese. Continue with the rest of the patties.

4. Place 1 teaspoon of marinara sauce and one patty on each bottom bun, then top with 1 tablespoon of marinara sauce and the top bun.

"The Brisket Was Great" (It's a Hanukkah Thing)

YIELD: 8 SERVINGS
PREP TIME: 15 MINUTES
COOK TIME:
5 TO 7 HOURS
GF

Inspired by: *The Holiday*

Sometimes the only way to get over a breakup is to put an ocean between you and the one who broke your heart. When Iris and Amanda swap houses for two weeks, Iris finds herself in LA, thousands of miles away from snowy London. While there, she gets a fresh start by connecting with new people, like Amanda's elderly neighbor Arthur, who asks her to host a dinner party so he can introduce her to his friends. It somehow turns into a Hanukkah thing, but that's okay because Iris slow-cooked a delicious brisket, perfect for the holiday. Turn any old dinner into a Hanukkah thing with this recipe, which pairs perfectly with macaroons—just make sure you give yourself enough time!

One 4- to 6-pound brisket

2 tablespoons kosher salt, divided

2 teaspoons freshly ground black pepper, divided

2 teaspoons dried oregano

1 teaspoon garlic powder

2 tablespoons olive oil

3 medium yellow onions, sliced

5 carrots, cut into 2-inch pieces

1 bunch celery, cut into 2-inch pieces

6 cloves garlic

2 cups beef broth

One 28-ounce can crushed tomatoes

¼ cup dark brown sugar

2 tablespoons red wine vinegar

2 bay leaves

SPECIAL TOOL:
Meat thermometer

1. Place the brisket in a roasting pan or on a wire rack on a rimmed baking sheet.

2. Preheat the oven to 300°F.

3. In a small bowl, mix together 1 tablespoon of salt, 1 teaspoon of pepper, and the oregano and garlic powder. Rub it all over the brisket.

4. In a large braiser or Dutch oven, add the olive oil and place on the stove over medium-high heat. Place the brisket in the braiser and sear for 5 minutes per side, rotating until all sides (including ends) have been browned. Remove the brisket and set aside on a separate rimmed baking sheet.

5. Add the onions, carrots, celery, and garlic to the braiser and cook for 6 to 7 minutes, stirring occasionally, until the vegetables are softened and browned.

6. Add the beef broth, crushed tomatoes, brown sugar, vinegar, the remaining salt and pepper, and bay leaves, and stir together. Bring to a boil and then reduce the heat to a simmer for 15 minutes, or until sauce thickens.

7. Fit the brisket back into the braiser, with the vegetables under and around it, and spoon some sauce onto the top of the meat. Cover and cook in the oven for 4 to 6 hours (about 1 hour per pound of meat) or until a thermometer in the largest part of the brisket reads 190°F.

8. Remove the brisket from the oven and let rest for 30 minutes. Cut against the grain into thin slices and serve with the vegetables and sauce.

First-Place Cake

Inspired by: *The Princess Switch*

YIELD: 2 CAKES
PREP TIME: 2 HOURS AND 45 MINUTES
COOK TIME: 30 MINUTES
V

When Stacey De Novo flies to the kingdom of Belgravia for its 56th annual Christmas baking competition, she finds herself in a princess-and-the-pauper situation with the crown prince's fiancée. Naturally, hijinks ensue. But there's no way she could have predicted someone would sabotage her mixer! Fortunately, you're welcome to use a mixer to make this more manageable version of the beautiful cake. You might not end up in a tiara, but this marvel of baking is deserving of a first-place prize!

RASPBERRY PURÉE:

12 ounces fresh or frozen raspberries

½ cup granulated sugar

¼ cup cornstarch

1 tablespoon water

1 tablespoon lemon juice

1 teaspoon vanilla extract

CAKE:

Oil or butter, for greasing

5 cups all-purpose flour, plus more for dusting

1½ tablespoons baking powder

1 teaspoon kosher salt

1½ cups unsalted butter, room temperature

3 cups granulated sugar

6 eggs, room temperature

1 tablespoon vanilla extract

2½ cups whole milk

Ingredients continued on page 92

TO MAKE THE RASPBERRY PUREE:

1. In a medium saucepan over medium heat, cook the raspberries and sugar for 8 to 10 minutes, stirring and mashing up the raspberries with a silicone spatula.

2. In a small bowl, mix together the cornstarch and water. Add to the saucepan and cook for 1 more minute or until slightly thickened. Remove from the heat and add the lemon juice and vanilla. Stir together and refrigerate the purée in a bowl until ready to use.

TO MAKE THE CAKE:

3. Preheat the oven to 350°F. Grease and flour three 8-inch round cake pans and four 6-inch round pans. (Don't have enough pans? You're not in a timed competition, so just bake the cakes in two batches.)

4. In a large bowl, mix the flour, baking powder, and salt. Set aside.

5. In the bowl of a stand mixer (or a large mixing bowl if using a hand mixer), beat the butter and sugar together on medium-high speed until light and fluffy, about 2 minutes. Add the eggs, mixing fully between each egg. Mix in the vanilla.

6. Mix half of the flour mixture into the butter mixture. Add half of the milk and mix. Continue with the rest of the flour mixture and milk. Make sure everything is fully mixed.

7. Pour the cake mix into each of the seven pans, filling them halfway.

8. Bake for 20 to 30 minutes, or until a toothpick inserted in the middle comes out clean. Timing will differ for the cakes in different-size pans, so be sure to check at 20 minutes and every 2 minutes after that.

9. Cool for 10 minutes in the pan, and then remove the cakes and cool completely on a wire rack, about 2 hours. (If you are baking the cakes in batches, you can clean and reuse the baking pans for the second round of cakes while the first batch is cooling.)

BUTTERCREAM FROSTING:

2 cups unsalted butter,
 room temperature

5⅓ cups powdered sugar,
 plus more for dusting

⅓ cup heavy cream (can also
 use heavy whipping cream)

3 teaspoons vanilla extract

⅛ teaspoon kosher salt

2 drops pink food coloring

CAKE DECORATION:

24 ounces red fondant,
 rolled out ⅛-inch thick

24 ounces white fondant, rolled
 out ⅛-inch thick

CHOCOLATE DRIZZLE:

1 cup semisweet chocolate chips

1 tablespoon vegetable shortening

Edible gold glitter

SPECIAL TOOL:

Piping bag with flat pastry tip

TO MAKE THE BUTTERCREAM FROSTING:

10. In the bowl of a stand mixer (or a large mixing bowl if using a hand mixer), beat the butter on medium-high speed until light and fluffy, about 2 minutes. Slowly add the powdered sugar, about ½ cup at a time, mixing fully each time. Add the cream, vanilla, salt, and pink food coloring and mix for 2 minutes or until everything is light, fluffy, and the texture of a thick buttercream frosting.

TO DECORATE THE CAKE:

11. Place the frosting into a piping bag with a flat pastry tip on the bottom. Place one 8-inch cake layer on a serving plate, pipe a layer of frosting on top, and cover with half of the raspberry purée Place the second 8-inch cake layer on top of the raspberry purée. Pipe a layer of frosting on top, and then place the third 8-inch cake layer on top. Frost the top and sides of the cake lightly with a "crumb coat," a thin layer of frosting to serve as a primer.

12. Sprinkle a work surface with powdered sugar; roll out the red and white fondant using more powdered sugar as needed to prevent sticking. Top the cake with the sheet of red fondant, slowly smoothing it down, ensuring it covers the full cake.

13. Place one 4-inch cake layer on a serving plate, pipe a layer of frosting on top, and cover with half of the remaining raspberry purée. Place the second 4-inch cake layer on top of the raspberry purée. Pipe a layer of frosting on top, and then place the third 4-inch cake layer on top. Top with the rest of the raspberry purée, and the final cake layer. Frost the top and sides of the cake lightly with a "crumb coat," a thin layer of frosting to serve as a primer.

14. Top the cake with the sheet of white fondant, slowly smoothing it down, ensuring it covers the full cake.

15. Place the 4-inch cake on top of the 8-inch cake.

16. Roll out some of the white fondant into a long piece, about 18 by 2 inches long and ⅛-inch thick. Use a pizza cutter or pastry wheel to cut into two ½-inch-wide strips. For one of the strips, in a very small dish, stir together 2 teaspoons of vodka and 1 teaspoon of gold luster dust. Use a clean artist's brush to paint one of the strips. Leave the other strip white. When the paint is dry, place the gold strip around the base of the red cake and the white strip around the base of the white cake. You can paint a little water on the cake to help the fondant pieces stick.

17. For a bow and poinsettias, roll out some red fondant to ⅛-inch thickness. To make the bow, cut some 1½-inch-wide strips. Shape the strips into two bow loops using pieces of cardboard tubes (from a paper towel roll) for support. Attach them together with a little water. Wrap the seam with another strip of fondant to make a bow. Cut the remaining strips of red fondant into two 5-inch-long tails for the bow. Let these bow pieces dry for several hours before removing the cardboard and placing on top of the cake.

18. Use a small poinsettia cutter to cut out shapes. Attach tiny gold balls with a little brush of water. Stick on the cake as desired. Cut ½-inch-wide strips of red fondant and place them on the white cake using a little water.

19. Place some frosting in a piping bag with a large star tip. Pipe stars along the edge of the top cake. Place a gold candy ball on each star.

TO MAKE THE CHOCOLATE DRIZZLE:

20. Melt the chocolate chips with vegetable shortening. Stir until smooth and let cool slightly. Drizzle over the edge of the red cake. Sprinkle the chocolate drizzle with some edible gold glitter. Serve slices to your most discerning judges.

2-FOR-1 PRETZELS

Inspired by: *Holidate*

The thing about romantic comedies is that they're all so *cockamamie*. We know that Sloane and her holidate, Jackson, are going to end up together, but not until they've experienced a year's worth of shenanigans, starting with their chance meeting at the mall. While there, they snagged a sweet 2-for-1 deal on pretzels, a great salty snack for taking the edge off another bad family holiday. Make your own pretzels, no coupon needed, and top them with Sloane's biggest vice: tons and tons of candy. Who cares if you don't have a date to share them with? That means more for you!

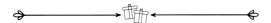

2¼ teaspoons (1 packet) active dry yeast

13½ cups plus 1 tablespoon warm water, divided

1 teaspoon granulated sugar

1 teaspoon kosher salt

1 tablespoon salted butter, melted

3¾ cups flour, plus more as needed

⅔ cup baking soda

1 egg

GARNISH:

Caramel sauce

Melted chocolate

Sprinkles

Small candies

1. In the bowl of a stand mixer (or a large mixing bowl if using a hand mixer), place the yeast, 1½ cups of warm water, and the sugar. Let dissolve together for 10 minutes.

2. Add the salt and butter to the mixture. Add the flour, 1 cup at a time, mixing with a dough hook attachment on low speed between each addition. Add more flour 1 tablespoon at a time as needed until the dough is no longer sticky.

3. Shape the dough into a ball, place it in a separate bowl, and cover for 30 minutes.

4. In the meantime, preheat the oven to 450°F. Line a baking sheet with parchment paper and set aside.

5. Once the oven has preheated, boil 12 cups of water and the baking soda together in a large pot over high heat.

6. Divide the dough into eight equal pieces. Roll each piece into a long rope, about 2 feet long, and then twist to make a pretzel shape: Create an upside-down "U," then twist the ends together twice and flip the ends up to the round part of the "U," going slightly past the "U" with the ends. Press gently to keep the pretzel's shape.

7. Drop each pretzel into the boiling water for 20 seconds. Place the boiled pretzels on the prepared baking sheet.

8. In a small bowl, mix the egg and the remaining 1 tablespoon of water together and brush over the pretzels.

9. Bake for 14 to 16 minutes or until browned. Drizzle caramel sauce and melted chocolate over the pretzels, then top with sprinkles and small candies.

chapter six

The Breakup and Makeup

Cue the torrential rain streaming down your windowpanes: You've just gone through a breakup. Don't worry, you'll get over it—but not until you complete the mandatory self-pity regimen. This grace period after your breakup requires all the ingredients that can mend a broken heart. That means put on your pajamas, get into bed, binge-eat your favorite junk food, and binge-watch all your favorite movies. The desserts in this section will lift anyone's spirits, and they all pair wonderfully with a pint of ice cream. So, delete your ex's number from your phone (if it's meant to be, they'll find their way back to you in Act 3) and get baking!

TIRAMISU ... YOU'LL SEE

Inspired by: *Sleepless in Seattle*

When recent widower and Seattle's Man of the Year Sam Baldwin decides to jump back in the dating pool for the first time since the Carter administration, he finds that a lot has changed. Tiramisu? What is that? The delicious, no-bake Italian dessert rose in popularity across the United States after this movie premiered, and if you try this recipe you'll see why: It's magic. This tiramisu is layered with delicate flavors of mascarpone, cocoa, and enough espresso to make you sleepless in Seattle. Easy to make but requiring some patience, this dessert will make any night an affair to remember.

4 egg yolks

½ cup granulated sugar

1 cup mascarpone cheese

¾ cup heavy whipping cream

1 teaspoon vanilla extract

1½ cups espresso, room temperature

3 tablespoons coffee-flavored liquor

24 ladyfingers

Cocoa powder, for dusting

1. Place the egg yolks and sugar into the bowl of a stand mixer with a whisk attachment (or a large mixing bowl if using a hand mixer). Mix on medium speed until very light and tripled in volume, 2 to 3 minutes. Add the mascarpone cheese and mix on medium speed until thoroughly combined.

2. In another large mixing bowl, place the cream and vanilla and whisk on medium speed until stiff peaks form, about 5 minutes. Fold the mascarpone-egg mixture into the cream mixture.

3. Pour the espresso and coffee liquor into a pie plate or other shallow rimmed dish. Roll the lady fingers through the liquid and lay half of them in a single layer on the bottom of an 8-by-8-inch square glass baking pan. Pour half of the remaining espresso-liquor mixture on top of the layer of ladyfingers.

4. Spread half of the mascarpone mixture over the ladyfingers and sift some cocoa powder on top. Add another layer of ladyfingers. Top with the rest of the mascarpone mixture and smooth.

5. Sift more cocoa powder onto the top of the tiramisu and refrigerate overnight before serving.

YIELD: 4 CRÈME BRÛLÉES
PREP TIME: 3 HOURS
COOK TIME: 40 MINUTES
V, GF

"IRRITATINGLY PERFECT" CRÈME BRÛLÉE

Inspired by: *My Best Friend's Wedding*

Speak now or forever hold your peace. Julianne Potter was enjoying the sweet, gelatin-like comfort of her marriage pact with her best friend, Michael O'Neal. If they were both still single by the time they turned twenty-eight, they'd marry each other. Enter Kimmy, Michael's fiancée, to ruin Julianne's plans. Kimmy is sweet. She's beautiful. She's irritatingly perfect. She's like a crème brûlée. And Julianne is ready to take a blowtorch to their wedding. If you're ever in a situation where you realize you're the villain in the love story, maybe give up on your destructive plan and channel your energy into cracking the crust on this perfect dessert.

2 cups heavy cream (can also use heavy whipping cream)

1 vanilla bean, split lengthwise, or 1 teaspoon vanilla extract

⅛ teaspoon salt

5 egg yolks

½ cup plus 2 tablespoons granulated sugar, divided

SPECIAL TOOLS:

Four 6-inch ramekins

Culinary torch

1. Preheat the oven to 325°F.

2. In a medium saucepan over medium heat, mix together the cream, vanilla, and salt. Cook until the cream begins to bubble, about 5 minutes. Turn off the heat, cover, and let sit for 5 minutes, then discard the vanilla bean, if using.

3. In a medium bowl, mix together the egg yolks and ½ cup of sugar until fully combined and light in color. Add the cream mixture slowly, about ¼ cup at a time, mixing between each addition. Give a final stir to ensure everything is combined.

4. Pour the crème brûlée mix into four 6-ounce ramekins. Place the ramekins in a large casserole dish and fill the dish with boiling water halfway up the sides of the ramekins.

5. Carefully move the casserole dish into the oven, and cook for 30 to 40 minutes, or until the centers of the crème brûlées are just barely set.

6. Move the ramekins to a wire rack to cool for 15 minutes, and then transfer to a refrigerator for at least 2 hours or until fully chilled.

7. Before serving, remove the crème brûlées from the refrigerator and let sit for 30 minutes, allowing them to come closer to room temperature. Sprinkle 1½ teaspoons of sugar on top of each ramekin and caramelize the sugar with a culinary torch until it makes a hardened crust over the custard.

YIELD: 3 COOKIE LOGS
(EACH LOG MAKES
18 COOKIES)
PREP TIME:
2 HOURS AND
15 MINUTES
COOK TIME: 10 MINUTES
V

"ALWAYS HAVE SOMETHING BAKING" COOKIE LOG

Inspired by: *Clueless*

According to love guru Cher Horowitz, you should always have something baking when a boy comes over. These homemade cookie logs are the perfect treat to have on hand for visitors. Between their aroma and the sounds of Mr. Billie Holiday wafting through the room, you'll land that Baldwin in no time. They're so easy to make, even a total space cadet could do it. Just, like, slice the dough, stick it in the oven, and soon the smell of warm chocolate chip cookies will fill your home. Make sure to check on them sporadically so they don't burn!

1 cup salted butter

1 cup packed brown sugar

½ cup granulated sugar

2 eggs

1 teaspoon vanilla extract

2½ cups all-purpose flour

½ teaspoon salt

¾ teaspoon baking soda

1 cup chocolate chips

1. In the bowl of a stand mixer (or a large mixing bowl if using a hand mixer), mix the butter on medium speed until it is light and creamy, 2 to 3 minutes, then mix in the brown sugar and granulated sugar.

2. One at a time, add the eggs followed by the vanilla, mixing fully in between each addition.

3. In a separate large mixing bowl, mix the flour, salt, and baking soda together, and then slowly add into the butter mixture until everything is fully mixed. Stir in the chocolate chips.

4. Separate the dough into three equal parts. One at a time, roll the dough onto a sheet of waxed paper until it is an evenly formed log about 8 to 10 inches long. Wrap the dough in the waxed paper and then wrap with plastic wrap. Repeat with the other two parts.

5. Refrigerate for at least 2 hours.

6. When ready to cook, unwrap the dough. Preheat the oven to 350°F and line two baking sheets with parchment paper. Slice each log with a large, sharp knife into ¼-inch rounds.

7. Place the cookie rounds 1 inch apart on the prepared baking sheets.

8. Bake for 10 minutes, or until the edges of the cookies are light brown and the cookies are firm but still slightly doughy.

9. Cool for 5 minutes and then transfer to a wire rack to finish cooling.

NOTE: Prefer to cook the full log in one go, Cher-style? Bake it for 30 to 35 minutes, rotating once halfway through. It'll be crispy and golden on the edges and still soft and gooey in the middle. If someone tells you to share it, just say, "As if!"

A Very, Very Good Brownie

Inspired by: *Notting Hill*

YIELD: 9 BROWNIES
PREP TIME: 35 MINUTES
COOK TIME: 35 MINUTES
V

Hollywood actress Anna Scott is just a girl, standing in front of a boy, asking for a shot at the last brownie, which is saved for the saddest act at the table of underachievers attending Honey's birthday dinner. The promise of a bite of these fudgy brownies has everyone clamoring to outdo one another's sob stories. Like Anna, these brownies are rich with a shiny veneer on the outside, and warm and soft on the inside. With an orange flavoring that calls back Anna and William Thacker's messy meet-cute, this dessert is very, very good.

Oil or butter, for greasing

½ cup unsalted butter

1 cup granulated sugar

2 eggs

1½ teaspoons vanilla extract

¾ cup all-purpose flour

½ cup cocoa powder

1 teaspoon orange zest

½ teaspoon baking powder

½ teaspoon salt

1. Preheat the oven to 350°F.

2. Grease a 9-inch square baking pan.

3. In a large saucepan over low heat, melt the butter, then add the sugar. Stir until smooth and then remove from the heat. Let cool for 2 minutes.

4. Add the eggs to the mixture one at a time, stirring between each addition. Stir in the vanilla.

5. In a small bowl, mix the flour, cocoa powder, orange zest, baking powder, and salt. Add this to the butter mixture and mix gently.

6. Pour the batter into the greased baking pan.

7. Bake for 30 to 35 minutes or until a toothpick inserted in the center comes out mostly clean (just a few crumbs).

8. Cool in the pan for 30 minutes.

9. Slice the brownies into square shapes and share with your friends.

Amélie's Famous Plum Cake

Inspired by: *Amélie*

The French have a saying, "Avoir les yeux plus gros que le ventre." Roughly translated, it means you'll want to pace yourself when faced with pastries. Make the lives around you a little better by sharing this plum kouign amann, a delicious Breton pastry made with laminated dough, and soon you may find that putting good out into the world pays out in *des dividends.* Just take care in setting up your mise en place before beginning, or you may learn, like Amélie, that you are out of one of the key ingredients. *Bon appetit!*

CAKE DOUGH:

1 tablespoon active dry yeast

¾ cup warm water

½ cup and 1 teaspoon granulated sugar, divided

2 cups all-purpose flour, plus more for the work surface

½ teaspoon kosher salt

Oil, for greasing

½ cup salted butter, chilled and cut into small cubes

CAKE TOPPING:

1 large plum, thinly sliced

2 tablespoons melted butter

2 tablespoons granulated sugar

TO MAKE THE CAKE DOUGH:

1. Place the yeast, warm water, and 1 teaspoon of sugar in the bowl of a stand mixer with a dough hook attachment (or a large mixing bowl if using a hand mixer). Let sit for 5 minutes, or until foamy.

2. Add the flour and salt to the mixing bowl. Mix together on low speed, and once combined, raise the speed to medium. Mix for 2 minutes or until dough becomes smooth and elastic.

3. Place the dough in an greased bowl and cover the bowl with plastic wrap. Let rise for 1 hour.

4. Take the dough out and place it on a lightly floured surface. Roll it into a rectangle about 12 by 18 inches.

5. Place the chilled butter in the center of the rectangle. Pour the remaining ½ cup of sugar over the butter. Fold each short side over the middle, covering the sugar and butter mixture, then seal the edges and lightly roll the dough flat with a rolling pin, and then fold the short sides into thirds again, making a thick square shape. Roll out one more time and then fold in the corners to make a smaller square. Repeat again.

6. Place the square of dough into a parchment paper-lined 9-inch cake pan. Cover with plastic wrap and let proof for 1 hour.

7. Preheat the oven to 425°F.

TO MAKE THE CAKE TOPPING:

8. Top the dough with the sliced plums, melted butter, and sugar.

9. Bake for 40 minutes or until golden and crusty.

10. Let cool for at least 15 minutes, then remove the cake from the pan.

Dr. Steve's Favorite Cookies

Inspired by: *The Wedding Planner*

Some people come into our lives and quickly go. Some people come into our lives and leave footprints on our heart. Some people come into our lives and point out that the brown M&M'S® taste better because they've got less artificial flavoring because chocolate's already brown, and then we can never untaste it. When pediatrician Steve Edison saves Mary Fiore from a runaway dumpster, they can't quite shake each other, especially because—surprise!—she's planning *his* wedding. Mary can't quite shake Steve's candy-eating preferences either, so she would love this recipe. These brown M&M'S cookies have even more chocolate and no additional artificial food coloring. Eat a couple, doctor's orders.

1 cup semisweet chocolate chips

½ cup unsalted butter

1½ cups flour

½ teaspoon baking soda

½ teaspoon salt

1 cup packed brown sugar

2 eggs

1 teaspoon vanilla extract

½ cup brown M&M'S

1. Preheat the oven to 350°F. Line a baking sheet with parchment paper and set aside.

2. Place the chocolate chips and butter in a microwave-safe bowl and microwave for 30 seconds. Stir and repeat until melted. Set aside.

3. In a small mixing bowl, whisk together the flour, baking soda, and salt.

4. In the bowl of a stand mixer (or a large mixing bowl if using a hand mixer), combine the brown sugar, eggs, and vanilla. Mix on medium speed until light and fluffy, about 1 minute.

5. Slowly add the melted chocolate to the sugar mixture and continue to mix on medium speed.

6. Add the flour mixture, mixing on low speed until just combined. Fold in the M&M'S.

7. Using a cookie scoop or a tablespoon, drop balls of cookie dough onto the prepared baking sheet, leaving 2 inches of space between each ball.

8. Bake for 9 to 12 minutes or until the cookies look cracked on top. Cool for 5 minutes on the baking sheet and then transfer to a wire rack.

NOTE: You don't have to stick with brown M&M'S for these cookies. The more colorful the better—just don't tell your doctor.

DANS LE NOIR STRAWBERRY MOUSSE

Inspired by: *About Time*

In the dark of Dans Le Noir restaurant, Tim meets Mary for the first time and quickly falls in love. Although many moments of his life will be redone, the fresh spontaneity of this chance meeting (and a bit of strawberry mousse in her eye) just adds to the beauty of the moment. Turn down the lights in your home for your own dining-in-dark adventure. Make sure you bookmark this recipe, because you'll want to experience it again and again.

¼ cup freeze-dried strawberries

½ cup granulated sugar, divided

4 ounces cream cheese, softened

1½ cups heavy cream (can also use heavy whipping cream)

½ tablespoon vanilla extract

SPECIAL TOOL:
Piping bag

1. Place the strawberries and ¼ cup of sugar in a food processor and process until fine and fully mixed.

2. In a large mixing bowl, beat the cream cheese and strawberry mixture together until smooth, about 2 minutes.

3. Place the heavy cream, vanilla, and remaining ¼ cup of sugar in a large mixing bowl. Beat with a whisk attachment on medium speed until stiff peaks form, about 6 minutes.

4. Gently mix half of the whipped cream mixture into the cream cheese mixture, and then mix in the rest, keeping it light and fluffy.

5. Place in a piping bag, snip off the bottom corner, and pipe about ½ cup mousse into six stemless martini glasses or small glass bowls.

TO ALL THE TURNOVERS I'VE LOVED BEFORE

Inspired by: *To All the Boys: P.S. I Still Love You*

Your first love always holds a special place in your heart. And, as Lara Jean knows, so does your first love triangle. So, when faced with difficult decisions in the romance department, do as Lara Jean would do—get in the kitchen and bake something sweet. These cherry turnovers are an elevated version of the toaster pastries you had as a kid, and the baking time will give you time to reminisce about all the boys you loved before.

3 cups all-purpose flour, plus more for the work surface

1 teaspoon kosher salt

4 tablespoons granulated sugar, divided

2 sticks unsalted butter, cold and cut into cubes

½ cup plus 1 tablespoon cold water, divided

8 ounces frozen cherries

1 tablespoon cornstarch

Juice from ½ lemon

2 eggs

3 tablespoons turbinado sugar

1. Preheat the oven to 375°F. Line a baking sheet with parchment paper and set aside.

2. In a large mixing bowl, mix together the flour, salt, and 1 tablespoon of sugar, and then cut in the butter with a pastry cutter or your hands. Combine until everything is fully mixed and slightly crumbly. Add ½ cup of cold water and mix again, then form into a ball.

3. Dust a large surface with flour and roll the dough out with a rolling pin until it's ⅛-inch thick.

4. Cut into 16 rectangles about 4 inches by 2 inches. You may need to cut 8, then roll out the remaining edges of dough again and cut out the rest. Place 8 rectangles on the baking sheet and cut 3 slits each in the other 8 rectangles, being careful not to cut all the way to the end. Set aside.

5. In a small saucepan over medium heat, mix the cherries, the remaining 3 tablespoons of sugar, the cornstarch, the remaining 1 tablespoon of cold water, and the lemon juice. Let simmer, stirring occasionally, for 3 minutes or until thickened.

6. Spoon 1½ tablespoons of filling into the center of each rectangle without slits. Top each with a slitted rectangle and crimp the edges with a fork.

7. Make an egg wash by whisking the eggs together and brushing the tops of each turnover. Sprinkle the tops with turbinado sugar. Bake for 20 to 25 minutes or until the turnovers are golden brown.

8. Let cool for 5 minutes, then transfer the turnovers to a wire rack to finish cooling.

Red, White, and Trifle Blue

Inspired by: *Red, White & Royal Blue*

Everyone knows opposites attract, and it doesn't get more opposite than all-American first son Alex and British Prince Henry. Alex and Henry's relationship is a slow burn that begins with one massive cake-tastrophe when they get in a row at a royal wedding and end up buried in white buttercream. With this recipe, you can repurpose the ruined cake into an elegant dessert along with other ingredients often found at weddings (like Champagne!). Your date will be chuffed with the elegant display, and the layering of sponge cake and custard will make this trifle an instant favorite.

CAKE:

2 cups all-purpose flour

2 cups granulated sugar

1 teaspoon baking soda

½ teaspoon kosher salt

1 cup unsalted butter

1 cup water

2 eggs

½ cup sour cream

1 teaspoon vanilla extract

CUSTARD:

5 egg yolks

⅓ cup granulated sugar

2½ tablespoons cornstarch

2½ cups whole milk

1 teaspoon vanilla extract

⅓ cup unsalted butter, cut into
   small pieces

Ingredients continued on page 116

1. Preheat the oven to 375°F and grease a 10-by-15-inch jelly roll pan or a 13-by-18-inch half-sheet baking pan.

TO MAKE THE CAKE:

2. Combine the flour, sugar, baking soda, and salt in a large bowl. Set aside.

3. Place the butter and water in a medium saucepan over medium-high heat and cook until it just begins to boil.

4. Remove from the heat, and then pour the butter mixture into the flour mixture. Mix together. Add the eggs, sour cream, and vanilla and stir until fully combined.

5. Pour the cake batter into the jelly roll pan or baking sheet and bake for 18 to 20 minutes, or until a toothpick inserted in the center comes out clean. While the cake is baking, make the custard.

TO MAKE THE CUSTARD:

6. In a medium bowl, mix together the egg yolks, sugar, and cornstarch. Set aside. Heat the milk in a small saucepan over medium-low heat, stirring frequently, until it just begins to simmer. Remove the milk from the stove and then very slowly, while whisking constantly, pour half of it into the egg mixture. Pour the egg-milk mixture back into the pot and heat over medium heat, whisking constantly until it begins to boil. Whisk while boiling for 1 to 2 minutes or until it has thickened. Remove the pot from heat, add the vanilla and butter, and whisk until the butter has melted and the mixture is smooth. Pour into a shallow bowl and cover with plastic wrap, touching the top of the custard.

7. Set the custard aside in the fridge to cool. When the cake comes out of the oven, let it sit and cool for 20 minutes. While the cake and custard are cooling, prepare the additional layers.

BERRY LAYERS:

2 cups sliced strawberries

2 cups blueberries

8 ounces champagne, divided

2 tablespoons granulated sugar, divided

WHIPPED CREAM:

1½ cups whipping cream

¼ cup powdered sugar

SPECIAL TOOL:

Trifle bowl

TO MAKE THE BERRY LAYERS:

8. Begin by macerating the berries. Place the strawberries and blueberries in separate small bowls and add 2 ounces of champagne and 1 tablespoon of sugar to each. Stir together until all berries are covered and set the bowls aside.

TO MAKE THE WHIPPED CREAM:

9. In the bowl of a stand mixer with a whisk attachment, whip the whipping cream and powdered sugar together until stiff peaks form, about 3 minutes.

TO ASSEMBLE THE TRIFLE:

10. Cut the cake into 2-inch cubes and place one layer of them (about one-third of the cake) at the bottom of a trifle bowl. Sprinkle 2 ounces of champagne over the cake. Top with the strawberries, then half of the custard and half of the whipped cream.

11. Repeat the layers, this time with the blueberries: cake topped with champagne, blueberries, custard, and whipped cream. (You may still have a little bit of cake left over.)

12. Smooth the top and chill until ready to serve. (The cake can be chilled for a couple hours up to a couple days.)

FROZEN HOT CHOCOLATE THAT'S "MEANT TO BE"

Inspired by: *Serendipity*

How *serendipitous* for you to land on this page! Clearly you were meant to make this frozen hot chocolate recipe, inspired by the one sold in NYC's Serendipity 3. Not yet sold, and want to test fate? Close this book and walk away. Next time you open the book, if you land on this recipe again, you know it's destiny. So, just in case, have some high-quality cocoa powder on hand. On second thought, take the chance and make it now. You could save yourself a lot of trouble, and who knows, you might just fall in love with it.

¼ cup cocoa powder

⅓ cup granulated sugar

⅓ cup dry milk powder

⅛ teaspoon kosher salt

3 cups ice

1¼ cups whole milk

½ cup whipped cream

Chocolate shavings, for garnish

1. Place the cocoa powder, sugar, milk powder, and salt in a blender and give it a couple quick pulses to mix together.

2. Add the ice and milk and blend until fully combined with a slushy consistency.

3. Pour into a goblet large enough for two people and top with whipped cream, chocolate shavings, and two straws and spoons for sharing.

chapter
seven

Happily Ever After

Picture this: You and the person you just *know* you're meant to be with are standing in the pouring rain, ready to confess your love to each another. No, wait—statistically you're probably more likely to be standing in an airport, out of breath after running through the terminal. Although, there's always a possibility you're at the top of the Empire State Building . . . forget it, it doesn't matter where you are. You found true love! You made it through all the misunderstandings and mishaps, the miscommunications and mistaken identities, the hijinks, and the bouts of amnesia. So go on—tell them that you love them and get ready to begin your happily ever after. Now, kiss!

SUPERB MYSTIC PIZZA

Inspired by: *Mystic Pizza*

YIELD: 2 PIZZAS
PREP TIME: 12+ HOURS
COOK TIME: 30 MINUTES
V

If there's one thing to love about a close-knit New England fishing town, it's the secret relationship drama that's always bubbling beneath the surface. If there's two things to love, it's the relationship drama . . . and the pizza! Yes, finding true love is nice, but finding the perfect pizza parlor is even better. Stop into Mystic Pizza for a pie that even the most ornery critic called "superb." The house special at the seaside pizza parlor has the exact right amount of cheese, tomatoes, and spices to make it truly mystic. The secret? Create one great recipe (below), and don't monkey with tradition.

PIZZA DOUGH:

3½ cups bread flour, plus more for dusting

1 teaspoon active dry yeast

1 teaspoon sugar

1 teaspoon kosher salt

2 cups lukewarm water

1 tablespoon olive oil, plus more for greasing

SAUCE:

One 28-ounce can whole peeled tomatoes (San Marzano preferred)

2 tablespoons olive oil

¼ cup minced yellow onion (about ½ onion)

3 cloves garlic, minced

2 teaspoons sugar

1 teaspoon kosher salt

1 teaspoon dried basil

½ teaspoon dried oregano

¼ teaspoon paprika

¼ teaspoon cumin

Ingredients continued on page 122

TO MAKE THE PIZZA DOUGH:

1. In a large bowl, combine the flour, yeast, sugar, and salt. Add the water and olive oil, mixing with your hands until fully combined.

2. Dust a work surface with flour and move the dough to the floured surface. Knead for 5 minutes, until the dough is smooth and elastic. (If the dough is too sticky, add more flour 1 tablespoon at a time.)

3. Place the dough into a greased bowl, cover with plastic wrap, and let rise in the refrigerator overnight.

TO MAKE THE SAUCE:

4. Pour the tomatoes into a large bowl and crush them by hand until a chunky sauce forms. Set aside.

5. Place the olive oil in a medium saucepan over medium heat and add the onions. Sauté until the onions are transparent, 2 to 3 minutes, then add the minced garlic. Cook for 2 minutes.

6. Add the crushed tomatoes, sugar, salt, basil, oregano, paprika, and cumin. Bring to a boil, then reduce the heat to low and let simmer for 30 minutes.

TO MAKE THE PIZZA:

7. Remove the dough from the refrigerator and cut it in half—you'll be making two pizzas.

8. Dust a pizza stone with flour, place it in the oven, and preheat the oven as high as it will go for 1 hour. (Most likely 500°F to 550°F.) Don't have a stone? Place a baking sheet in the oven while it preheats.

PIZZA:

Flour, for the work surface

Oil, for greasing (optional)

16 ounces whole-milk, low-moisture mozzarella, cut into ½-inch cubes

¼ cup sliced mushrooms (about 5 mushrooms)

½ green bell pepper, sliced

SPECIAL TOOL:

Pizza peel (optional)

9. Take one dough ball and place it onto a floured surface. With floured hands, slowly stretch the disk into a large circle by holding one edge and continuing to rotate along the edge, letting gravity stretch it downward. Continue until the pizza crust is 12 to 14 inches in diameter and even in thickness.

10. Place the pizza crust onto a pizza peel (or grease the preheated baking sheet with oil).

11. Place ¾ cup of sauce in the middle of the pizza crust and use the back of a spoon to lightly spread it around the rest of the crust, leaving a ½-inch border around the edge. Sprinkle half of the cheese evenly on top of the sauce, then top with half of the mushrooms and half of the green bell pepper slices.

12. Transfer the pizza onto the pizza stone and bake for 12 to 15 minutes, or until the crust is brown and the cheese is melted and beginning to brown.

13. Remove the pizza from the oven and onto a cutting board. Let sit for a few minutes and cut into four large pieces.

14. To make the second pizza, repeat steps 8 through 12.

CAMMARERI BROS. BAKERY FULL MOON BREAD

Inspired by: *Moonstruck*

Sometimes it happens at the most inopportune moment: You meet someone at the wrong place, wrong time, but sparks fly, and there's nothing you can do to stop it. You're moonstruck. Like Loretta and her family and friends— the Castorinis, the Cammareris, the Cappomagis—you have to sift through the chemistry, the passion, and the *amore* to find something everlasting. This cheese-covered loaf honors both the bright moon that fills the sky during the couple's courtship and the Cammareri Bros. Bakery. Bake a fresh loaf and share it with a loved one. Bread is life, after all. And, remember, life is full of chaos, distractions, and interruptions, so please be careful around the bread slicer.

3 cups all-purpose flour, plus more for the work surface

½ teaspoon instant yeast

2 teaspoons kosher salt

1½ cups lukewarm water

1 cup shredded pepper jack cheese, divided

1. In a large bowl, combine the flour, yeast, and salt. Add the water and stir until fully mixed, then incorporate ½ cup of shredded cheese. (The dough will be sticky.)

2. Cover the bowl with plastic wrap and let rest at room temperature for 12 hours. The dough will bubble up and rise.

3. Place a Dutch oven or other large oven-safe pot with a lid in the oven and preheat the oven to 450°F. Keep the pot in the oven for 30 minutes.

4. While the oven and pot are heating, sprinkle flour over a cutting board or other work surface, then turn the dough out onto the surface. Gently form a ball with the dough and loosely cover it with plastic wrap.

5. When the 30 minutes is up, carefully remove the Dutch oven. Uncover the bread and place it on a sheet of parchment paper. Lift the parchment paper with the dough on it, place it into the Dutch oven, and cover the pot.

6. Bake for 30 minutes. Then remove the lid, cover the top of the loaf with the remaining ½ cup of shredded cheese, forming a large moon-shaped circle, and bake for another 10 minutes.

7. Remove from the oven and cool the bread on a wire rack.

THE PERFECT BITE

YIELD: 12 SKEWERS
PREP TIME: 7 MINUTES
COOK TIME: 5 MINUTES
GF

Inspired by: *The Mirror Has Two Faces*

When you want your love story to end on the right note, it's good to embrace rituals, particularly when it results in a harmoniously balanced, perfect bite. Though your own culinary customs may not be as particular as Rose Morgan's ("Rotate the plate counterclockwise, cut on the diagonal . . ."), these skewers offer a great opportunity to build your own ideal mouthful of meat, cheese, and salad–inspired produce. Adjust the ingredients to your liking so you always end on the perfect bite!

ITALIAN DRESSING:

¼ cup extra-virgin olive oil

1½ tablespoons red vinegar

½ tablespoon lemon juice

¼ teaspoon dried oregano

⅛ teaspoon dried thyme

⅛ teaspoon dried basil

⅛ teaspoon garlic powder

⅛ teaspoon salt

⅛ teaspoon granulated sugar

Dash freshly ground black pepper

⅛ tablespoon grated Parmesan cheese

CHICKEN:

1 chicken breast

1 tablespoon extra-virgin olive oil

½ teaspoon kosher salt

¼ teaspoon freshly ground black pepper

¼ teaspoon paprika

3 leaves romaine heart

6 cherry tomatoes

12 mozzarella balls

1 avocado

SPECIAL TOOLS:

Twelve 3-inch skewers

TO MAKE THE ITALIAN DRESSING:

1. In a small bowl, whisk together the olive oil, red vinegar, lemon juice, oregano, thyme, basil, garlic powder, salt, sugar, a dash of black pepper, and Parmesan. Set aside.

TO MAKE THE CHICKEN:

2. Cut the chicken breast into 1-inch cubes and place in a large bowl with the olive oil, salt, pepper, and paprika. Mix until the chicken is well coated.

3. In a medium pan over medium-high heat, sauté the chicken until fully cooked, about 5 minutes. Remove from the heat and set aside.

4. Cut the romaine leaves into 1-inch squares and cut the cherry tomatoes in half. Place the lettuce and tomatoes in a small bowl with the mozzarella balls. Add 2 tablespoons of the Italian dressing and mix until well coated.

5. Cut the avocado in half, removing the pit and peeling the flesh away from the peel. Cut the avocado into 1-inch squares and set aside.

6. Using 3-inch skewers, add one of each item to compile the "perfect bite": the cherry tomato, then romaine, avocado, chicken, and mozzarella.

7. Drizzle additional Italian dressing over the skewers ("Just glop it on!") and serve.

ALWAYS BE MY KIMCHI

Inspired by: *Always Be My Maybe*

Sometimes a relationship needs time to sit before you can enjoy it, like when Sasha and Marcus give their relationship sixteen years to pickle before finding their way back to each other in the end. Celebrity chef Sasha Tran may have fancy restaurants across the country, but her love of cooking came from eating the traditional Korean dishes made by Marcus's mom, Judy. This kimchi jjigae, made Judy's way, ignited Sasha's desire to make food for others and inspired her most intimate restaurant. Make a pot of this to share with your family, friends, loves, "maybes," and, yes, even Keanu Reeves.

1 tablespoon canola oil

¾ cup old kimchi, cut into ½-inch pieces

¼ pound pork belly, sliced thin and cut into ½-inch pieces

½ medium yellow onion, sliced

1 teaspoon gochugaru (chile flakes)

1 teaspoon minced garlic (about 2 cloves)

¼ cup kimchi brine

2 cups chicken broth

7 ounces firm tofu, sliced into ¼-inch-thick rectangles

2 green onions, sliced on the diagonal in ¼-inch pieces

2 cups cooked white rice, for serving

1. Heat the oil in a medium saucepot over medium-high heat. Add the kimchi, pork belly, onion, gochugaru, and garlic and cook until the kimchi is softened and the pork is cooked through, 5 to 7 minutes.

2. Add the kimchi brine and chicken broth and bring to a boil. Reduce the heat to medium, cover, and simmer for 15 minutes.

3. Add the tofu and simmer for another 5 minutes or until the tofu is heated through. Pour into bowls, garnish with green onion, and serve with a bowl of white rice on the side.

BRIDGET'S BIRTHDAY BLUE SOUP

Inspired by: *Bridget Jones's Diary*

YIELD: 4 SERVINGS
PREP TIME: 5 MINUTES
COOK TIME: 40 MINUTES
V, GF

If you want a guaranteed happy ending, simply surround yourself with brilliant friends. Nobody's perfect, but Bridget Jones is uniquely imperfect, and as far as her friends are concerned, it's part of her charm. And just as charming is her leek soup, boldly displaying an unusual pastel blue color not typically found in nature. You can make your own version of Bridget's blue leek soup for your next dinner party. Even if you choose not to add the blue food coloring, you will love it, just as it is.

2 tablespoons salted butter

5 medium russet potatoes, peeled and roughly chopped

3 large leeks, washed and thinly sliced

1 celery, diced

2 cloves garlic, minced

6 cups vegetable broth

½ cup heavy cream (can also use heavy whipping cream)

1 teaspoon kosher salt

1 drop blue food coloring, plus more as needed

SPECIAL TOOLS:

Immersion blender

Baker's twine

1. Heat the butter in a large pot over medium heat. Add the potatoes, leeks, celery, and garlic and cook, stirring occasionally, for 8 to 10 minutes or until the vegetables are softened and browned.

2. Add the vegetable broth and bring to a boil. Cover, reduce the heat to low, and simmer for 30 minutes.

3. Remove from the heat and use an immersion blender to blend until smooth.

4. Add the cream, salt, and blue food coloring. Stir. Add more blue food coloring, if needed.

5. Divide into four bowls and serve. Garnish with baker's twine (only joking, of course).

"Make a Wish…" Birthday Cake

Inspired by: *Sixteen Candles*

Turning sweet sixteen isn't as great as everyone makes it out to be. Being a teenager is tough! You're sorting through social situations, surging with hormones, and feeling conspicuous and invisible at the same time. Worse, you're not sure your crush knows you're alive. Even *worse*, you're not even sure your *family* knows you're alive. Cheer yourself up with the perfect birthday cake. This moist, rich chocolate cake with layers of frosting and sprinkles can turn even the worst birthday around. Add a touch of pretty pink food coloring to the buttercream frosting to make it look like Sam's iconic birthday cake. No need to make a wish when you blow out these candles. It's already come true.

CAKE:

½ cup canola oil, plus more for greasing

2 cups all-purpose flour, plus more for the cake pans

2 cups granulated sugar

1 cup cocoa powder

2 teaspoons baking soda

1 teaspoon baking powder

1 teaspoon kosher salt

1 cup buttermilk

2 eggs

2 teaspoons vanilla extract

¾ cup black coffee, room temperature

FROSTING:

1½ cups unsalted butter, room temperature

6 cups powdered sugar

¼ cup heavy cream (can also use heavy whipping cream)

2 teaspoons vanilla extract

⅛ teaspoon kosher salt

1 to 2 drops pink food coloring

¼ cup rainbow sprinkles

Ingredients continued on page 132

TO MAKE THE CAKE:

1. Preheat the oven to 350°F. Grease and flour two 9-inch cake pans.

2. In the bowl of a stand mixer (or in a large mixing bowl if using a hand mixer), mix the flour, sugar, cocoa powder, baking soda, baking powder, and salt on low speed. Add the buttermilk and oil slowly while continuing to mix on low speed. Add the eggs to the batter, mixing fully between each addition. Mix in the vanilla followed by the coffee, making sure everything is fully mixed.

3. Pour half of the cake mix into each prepared cake pan.

4. Bake for 30 minutes, or until a toothpick inserted in the middle comes out clean.

5. Cool for 10 minutes in the pans, and then remove the cakes from the pans and cool completely, about 2 hours, on a wire rack.

TO MAKE THE FROSTING:

6. While the cake is cooling, beat the butter on medium speed in the bowl of a stand mixer (or a large bowl if using a hand mixer) until light and fluffy, 2 to 3 minutes. Slowly add the powdered sugar, ½ cup at a time, mixing fully each time. Add the cream, vanilla, and salt and mix for 2 minutes or until everything is light, fluffy, and the texture of a thick buttercream frosting.

7. Take one-third of the frosting and it place in a small bowl with the pink food coloring. Mix until color is uniform.

8. Place the white frosting into a piping bag with a flat pastry tip on the bottom, and the pink frosting into a piping bag with a star tip.

SPECIAL TOOLS:

Piping bag with a flat pastry tip

Piping bag with a star tip

9. Place one cake layer on a serving plate and pipe a layer of white frosting on top. Add sprinkles to the top of the frosting.

10. Place the second cake layer on top of the sprinkled frosting. Pipe a layer of white frosting on the top and sides of the cake. Using a silicone spatula, even out the frosting along the cake. Chill the cake for 30 minutes or until the base layer of frosting has firmed.

11. Use the pink frosting to pipe around the top and bottom edges of the cake, and pipe swirls along the side of the cake. Top with 16 pink candles.

LEGALLY BLONDIES

Inspired by: *Legally Blonde*

YIELD: 16 BLONDIES
PREP TIME: 10 MINUTES
COOK TIME: 25 MINUTES
V

Sometimes the happiest ending is the one where you fall in love with yourself. When you're suffering from a broken heart, you'll go to any lengths to win back the love of your life. Even though you know it would serve you better to focus on yourself for a while. Get your nails done. Read a book. Maybe go to law school? While you're there, you can whip up a treat for your study group. These blondies have a swirl of Elle Woods's signature pink—they'll give you endorphins, and endorphins make you happy. No matter what your boneheaded ex thinks, you're smart and competent, so even if you're not a professional baker you'll be able to make these treats in a bend and snap. What, like it's hard?

½ cup butter, melted, plus more for the baking pan

1 cup flour, plus more for the baking pan

½ teaspoon salt

¾ cup packed brown sugar

1 egg

1½ teaspoons vanilla extract

3 ounces ruby chocolate

1. Preheat the oven to 350°F. Grease an 8-by-8-inch baking pan with butter. Dust with flour and tap out the excess.

2. In a small bowl, mix together the flour and salt. Set aside.

3. In a large mixing bowl, mix together the melted butter and brown sugar. Add the egg and vanilla and mix until fully combined. Slowly add the flour mixture and mix just until combined.

4. Spread the batter evenly into the baking pan.

5. In a microwave-safe bowl, melt the ruby chocolate by microwaving in 30-second intervals, stirring in between.

6. Drizzle the melted chocolate in long lines across the batter. Swirl it by dragging a butter knife through the chocolate perpendicular of the lines.

7. Bake for 25 minutes or until a toothpick inserted in the center comes out clean.

8. Let cool on a wire rack and then cut into 16 equal squares.

Post-Credits Scene

The movie screen has faded to black. Now what? The misunderstandings have been sorted out and the plot resolved, leaving you with the realities of day-to-day life. Cue the post-credits scene! Grand gestures are romantic, but this snapshot shows that love is really about the mundane moments, like sharing an afternoon picnic or stealing a glance at each other from across the room at a bustling cocktail party. Put together a compilation of some favorite clips to make a perfect menu for any post-credits scene.

AFTERNOON PICNIC

Celebrate a sunny day with this easy-to-pack picnic. Kick things off with a refreshing rum drink while you and you and your fellow picnic attendees choose between sandwiches: egg salad or swoon-worthy turkey. Premade chicken skewers offer a balanced meal on a stick, whereas M&M'S-enhanced cookies are not only delicious, they also travel well. Just watch out for ants.

+ What She's Having (page 11)

✗ Egg Salad Obsession (page 75)

+ The Perfect Bite (page 125)

+ Dr. Steve's Favorite Cookies (page 109)

GIRLS' NIGHT IN

Get out the movies, magazines, and mud masks—it's a girls' night in! Start out with a frothy blended daiquiri and dig into some truly superb pizza. Stick a Cher-proof cookie log in the oven while munching on premade blondies. And if the night goes long, have supplies on hand to whip up some late-night sandwiches.

+ Thirteen Going on Thirty, Flirty & Thriving Daiquiri (page 39)

+ Superb Mystic Pizza (page 121)

+ "Always Have Something Baking" Cookie Log (page 103)

COCKTAIL PARTY

As your guests arrive, wow them with a charcuterie board worthy of a treasure hunt, accompanied by a choice of delicious cocktails: a fruity martini or a potent Scotch drink. Midparty, pass some "killer" seafood nibbles around on a platter, and then end the night with freshly flamed mini crème brûlées.

+ The Lost City of D(eliciousness) Charcuterie (page 25)

+ Poisonous Apple Martini: One Sip Is All It Takes (page 41)

+ The Colonial Woman (page 35)

+ "Death on a Leaf!" (page 23)

+ "Irritatingly Perfect" Crème Brûlée (page 101)

BRUNCH WITH THE FAMILY

If you must prepare a feast for your family, you won't go wrong with this menu. Whether your guests want Roman-style coffee or a boozy Breakfast of Champions, you're covered. Make the scones and cinnamon rolls in advance, so your family can dig in while you make the croque monsieurs. Bon Appetit!

✦ Roman Holiday Caffé: The Shakerato (page 47)

✦ Breakfast of Champions (page 61)

✦ Rule #23 Scones (page 53)

✦ The PropROLLsal: Living in Sin-namon Rolls (page 57)

✦ It's (Not Too) Complicated Croque Monsieur (page 65)

✦ Legally Blondies (page 133)

✦ White Christmas Platter: Late-Night Sandwiches (page 79)

DINNER DATE

Impress your date with this classy dinner: Make the bread and strawberries in advance and have the rack of lamb in the oven when they arrive. Shake together a couple cozy cocktails and nibble on some bread until the lamb is finished. When you're done with your meal, serve chilled, boozy strawberries for your nightcap.

✗ You've Got Cocktail: New York in the Fall (page 37)

✦ Cammareri Bros. Bakery Full Moon Bread (page 123)

✦ Mary's Little Rack of Lamb (page 21)

✦ "Bring Out the Flavor" Champagne Strawberries (page 33)

Dietary Considerations

V: VEGETARIAN ♡ V*: EASILY MADE VEGETARIAN ♡ V+: VEGAN ♡ V+*: EASILY MADE VEGAN
GF: GLUTEN FREE ♡ GF*: EASILY MADE GLUTEN FREE

CHAPTER ONE: MEAT-CUTE

What She's Having

Rosie's Meatballs

My Big Fat Greek "~~Mooseeaca~~" Moussaka

Prepare to Dine: Fezzik's Stew (*The Princess Bride*)

3 Lemon Centerpiece-of-Chicken

Mary's Little Rack of Lamb . . . . **GF**

"Death on a Leaf!"

The Lost City of D(eliciousness) Charcuterie

CHAPTER TWO: LET'S MEET FOR DRINKS

Dirty Mixing: "I Carried a Watermelon" Cocktail . . . . **V, V+, GF***

The Ding-a-Ling . . . . **V, V+, GF***

"Bring Out the Flavor" Champagne Strawberries. . . . . **V, V+, GF**

The Colonial Woman. . . . . **V, V+, GF***

You've Got Cocktail: New York in the Fall . . . . **V, V+, GF***

Thirteen Going on Thirty, Flirty and Thriving Daiquiri . . . . **V*, V+*, GF***

Poisonous Apple Martini: One Sip is All it Takes. . . . . **V, V+, GF***

Your Glass or Mine: Garden Glory . . . . **V, V+, GF**

CHAPTER THREE: THE MORNING AFTER

Roman Holiday Caffè: The Shakerato . . . . **V, V+, GF**

Breakfast at Tiffany's. . . . . **V**

Date #50 Waffles . . . . **V**

Rule #23 Scones . . . . **V**

Beignet and the Jets . . . . **V**

The PropROLLsal: Living in Sin-namon Rolls . . . . . . **V**

Forever February Breakfast Cake . . . . **V**

Breakfast of Champions. . . . . **V, V+, GF**

CHAPTER FOUR: LONG-TERM RELATIONSHIP

It's (Not Too) Complicated Croque Monsieur

10 Things I Hate Pad See Ew

Eat, Pray, and Eat Some More

Crazy Rich Dumplings

She's Ball That: Supersized Falafel Balls . . . . . **V, V+, GF**

Egg Salad Obsession . . . . **V**

Measurement Conversions

Kitchen Measurements

CUPS	TABLESPOONS	TEASPOONS	FLUID OUNCES
1⁄16 cup	1 tablespoon	3 teaspoons	½ fluid ounce
⅛ cup	2 tablespoons	6 teaspoons	1 fluid ounce
¼ cup	4 tablespoons	12 teaspoons	2 fluid ounces
⅓ cup	5⅓ tablespoons	16 teaspoons	2⅔ fluid ounces
½ cup	8 tablespoons	24 teaspoons	4 fluid ounces
⅔ cup	10⅔ tablespoons	32 teaspoons	5⅓ fluid ounces
¾ cup	12 tablespoons	36 teaspoons	6 fluid ounces
1 cup	16 tablespoons	48 teaspoons	8 fluid ounces

GALLON	QUART	PINT	CUP	CUP
1⁄16 gallon	¼ quart	½ pint	1 cup	8 fluid ounces
⅛ gallon	½ quart	1 pint	2 cups	16 fluid ounces
¼ gallon	1 quart	2 pints	4 cups	32 fluid ounces
½ gallon	2 quarts	4 pints	8 cups	64 fluid ounces
1 gallon	4 quarts	8 pints	16 cups	128 fluid ounces

Oven Temperatures

CELCIUS	FARENHEIT
93°C	200°F
103°C	225°F
121°C	250°F
135°C	275°F
149°C	300°F
163°C	325°F
177°C	350°F
191°C	375°F
204°C	400°F
218°C	425°F
232°C	450°F

Weight

GRAMS	OUNCES
142 grams	5 ounces
170 grams	6 ounces
283 grams	10 ounces
397 grams	14 ounces
454 grams	16 ounces
907 grams	32 ounces

Length

IMPERIAL	METRIC
1 inch	2.5 centimeters
2 inches	5 centimeters
4 inches	10 centimeters
6 inches	15 centimeters
8 inches	20 centimeters
10 inches	25 centimeters
12 inches	30 centimeters

Fry Station Safety Tips

If you're making something that requires deep frying, here are some important tips to prevent any kitchen fires:

✦ If you don't have a dedicated deep fryer, use a Dutch oven or a high-walled sauté pan.

✦ Never have too much oil in the pan! You don't want hot oil spilling out as soon as you put the food in.

✦ Only use a suitable cooking oil, like canola, peanut, or vegetable oil.

✦ Always keep track of the oil temperature with a thermometer—350°F to 375°F should do the trick.

✦ Never put too much food in the pan at the same time!

✦ Never put wet food in the pan. It will splatter and may cause burns.

✦ Always have a lid nearby to cover the pan in case it starts to spill over or catch fire. A properly rated fire extinguisher is also great to have on hand in case of emergencies.

✦ Never leave the pan unattended and never let children near the pan.

✦ Never, ever touch the hot oil.

Glossary

COOKING TERMS

BEAT: To blend ingredients and/or incorporate air into a mixture by vigorously whisking, stirring, or using a handheld or stand mixer.

BIAS CUT: A diagonal cut often used for vegetables. Hold the item at a slight angle as you slice.

CRIMP: To seal together the edges of two pieces of pastry dough by pressing the dough with the tines of a kitchen fork, the side of a knife, or a pastry crimper. Crimping can be used to securely seal together the uncooked crusts of a double-crust pie, which may then be fluted if desired.

EGG WASH: A mixture used to create a sheen or gloss on breads, pastries, and other baked goods. Whisk together one egg and 1 tablespoon of water until light and foamy. Use a pastry brush to apply before baking when the recipe requires.

FOLDING IN: To gently add an ingredient with a silicone spatula in wide gentle strokes. Do not whisk or stir vigorously. Folding allows any airiness already established to stay intact.

FRENCHED: To trim the meat (usually lamb) off a shank to give it a "lollipop" feel that allows you to pick it up with your hands. You can ask a butcher to make this cut for you.

GREASING A PAN: To coat a pan with nonstick cooking spray, oil, softened butter, or shortening to keep (usually) baked goods such as cakes from sticking.

KNEAD: To uncover the dough and use the heel of one hand to push the dough away from you and then pull it back with your fingertips. Turn and repeat until the dough is smooth and elastic, 5 to 7 minutes.

MINCE: To gather the ingredient together and rock a knife blade over it until it is cut into small, even pieces (finely chopped) or as finely as possible (minced).

PIPING FROSTING: To decorate cakes and cookies by squeezing frosting placed in a decorating bag over them. Piping can be done with or without a decorating tip—or even in a plastic bag with one corner snipped off to allow the frosting to be applied in a neat rope shape.

REDUCE: To simmer or boil a liquid, such as broth or wine, in order to enhance its flavor. As the quantity of the liquid decreases, the liquid thickens into a flavorful sauce.

RISE: The process by which yeasted breads gain structure and height, or "rise" and grow. This is often done at room temperature over a couple hours, but sometimes is done in the refrigerator or overnight.

ROAST: To cook in an uncovered roasting pan, which intensifies flavors. Because the oven does most of the work, this technique requires little hands-on cooking time. Before you start, line a heavy roasting pan with aluminum foil and brush the foil with a little olive oil to help prevent sticking.

SAUTÉ: To cook quickly in a small amount of fat. The pan should be preheated with fat before adding foods so that they sear quickly, and there should be plenty of room in the pan so that foods don't get crowded and simmer in their own juices.

SEAR: To create a crust on a piece of meat, poultry, or fish by placing it in a very hot pan or on a very hot grill. The high heat quickly caramelizes the natural sugars in the food, creating a deeply browned and flavorful crust. Once the crust is formed, the heat is usually turned down so that the interior of the meat can cook properly before the outside burns.

SIMMER: To cook a liquid over a stovetop at a low heat so that it maintains consistent, medium-to-small bubbles while cooking liquids over a stovetop. This is often achieved by bringing the liquid to a boil, then reducing the heat to low and covering.

WHIP: To use a whisk or electric mixer to aerate ingredients such as egg whites and heavy whipping cream, causing them to lighten, stiffen, and form peaks.

INGREDIENTS

ACTIVE DRY YEAST: Available in ¼-ounce (7 gram) packages containing 2¼ teaspoons yeast. Be sure to check the date on the package to make sure the yeast is truly active. Contrary to what the package says, you don't have to use warm water.

CAKE FLOUR: Milled from soft wheat and containing cornstarch, cake flour is low in protein and high in starch. It gives cakes a light crumb. Cake flour has also undergone a bleaching process that increases its ability to hold water and sugar, so cakes made with cake flour are less likely to fall.

COOKING UTENSILS

BAKING DISH: Shallow, rectangular dishes made of tempered glass, porcelain, or earthenware. These all-purpose vessels work for roasting meat or vegetables and baking brownies or bread pudding. Items will cook more slowly in opaque ceramic than they will in clear glass.

BAKING PAN: Use these pans, which typically measure 13 by 9 inches with sides 2 to 2½ inches high, for baking sheet cakes, brownies, corn bread, and coffee cakes. You can also use these pans for making casseroles.

BAKING SHEET: A baking sheet (also called a sheet pan) is a rectangular metal pan with shallow, slightly sloping rims. Choose sturdy stainless-steel ones that will last for years.

BLENDER: Used to blend or purée sauces and soups to varying textures, from chunky to perfectly smooth, and to make smoothies and shakes.

CAKE PAN: Round pans, generally 2 inches deep and 8 or 9 inches in diameter, used especially for baking cakes. You will want to have at least two on hand for making layer cakes.

CANDY THERMOMETER: Sometimes called fry thermometers, these long glass thermometers can be clipped to the side of a pot. They can withstand temperatures of at least 500°F and are used to measure the temperatures of frying oil or sugar when making syrups, candies, and certain frostings.

DOUGH HOOK: An attachment for a stand mixer used for making bread doughs. Most of the various types of dough hooks manage to knead dough well. However, the size of the bowl is important. Surprisingly, many stand mixers come with a bowl that is too small, so if you are going to bake large amounts, carefully check the details when purchasing one.

DRY MEASURING CUPS: Measuring tools that usually come in sizes of ¼ cup, ⅓ cup, ½ cup, and 1 cup. They are ideal for measuring dry ingredients such as flour, sugar, rice, and pasta.

DUTCH OVEN: A large heavy cooking pot usually made of cast iron. You can cook with a Dutch oven on the stove and in the oven. Dutch ovens are great at retaining heat, making them the perfect cooking vessel for just about everything.

HIGH-HEAT vs. NONSTICK PANS: A high-heat pan—as its name suggests—can be used to cook at temperatures between 400°F and 600°F. They're usually made of stainless steel, cast iron or enameled cast iron and can be used on the stovetop or oven (if the handle is made of an ovenproof material). Nonstick cookware contains a coating that helps keep foods from sticking (particularly eggs), but they can't be used at the same temperatures as high-heat pans. If you are cooking with nonstick cookware, make sure you know the manufacturer's heat limits for your cookware. Most nonstick cookware should not be used at above medium heat on a stovetop (about 350°F) and is not generally suitable for the oven.

IMMERSION BLENDER: Also called hand or handheld blenders, immersion blenders have an extended blade that is immersed in a food or mixture to blend or purée it. Immersion blenders are great for puréeing food in the container in which it is mixed or cooked. This means that they can blend larger amounts of food than a standing blender. Immersion blenders can be used to make a frothy foam on creamed soups. These blenders usually have only two speeds, and the blade must be completely immersed in the food to prevent spattering. Some have whisk attachments or small containers for blending small amounts of food.

LIQUID MEASURING CUP: These clear glass or plastic cups are used for measuring precise amounts of liquids. Useful sizes include 1 cup, 2 cup, and 4 cup.

MEASURING SPOONS: A set of measuring tools used to accurately portion smaller amounts of ingredients. They usually come in a set that includes ⅛ teaspoon, ¼ teaspoon, ½ teaspoon, 1 teaspoon, and 1 tablespoon. Use them for liquid ingredients such as vinegar, juices, oils, and extracts, as well as dry ingredients such as flour, salt, sugar, and spices.

MEAT THERMOMETER: Every kitchen should have a meat thermometer. There are two kinds: a probe type, which is inserted into the meat at the beginning of cooking and left there until the proper temperature is reached; and an instant-read type, which is inserted toward the end of the cooking period to test for doneness. To use, insert in the center of a piece of meat or a roast, or on the inside of the thickest part of the thigh of a bird; make sure the thermometer is not touching bone.

MIXER: Two basic types of motor-driven electric mixers are available: stand (or standing) and handheld (or portable), and each has its place in the kitchen. Stand mixers are stationary machines good for large amounts of ingredients and heavy batters.

PARING KNIFE: A small, evenly proportioned blade usually 3 to 4 inches long. It's used for paring, peeling, and slicing fruits and vegetables, and for chopping small quantities.

PASTRY BAG: A cone-shaped bag used to pipe frosting or icing on cakes, cookies, cupcakes, and other desserts. These bags come in disposable and reusable options and usually come with a set of attachable tips to create different frosting shapes. Some disposable options are microwave-safe, which is useful for melting chocolate or other items (be sure to check the packaging before trying this). They can also be used to pipe batter, dough, creams, or puréed ingredients ahead of cooking.

SAUTÉ PAN: Sauté pans have high, angled handles and relatively high sides to help prevent food from bouncing out of the pan when stirred, turned, or flipped. The sides can range from 2½ to 4 inches high, with 3 inches being the most popular. Sauté pans can measure from 6 to 14¼ inches in diameter, and volume capacities generally range from 1 to 7 quarts, with 2½ to 4 quarts being the most useful for home cooks. They often come with lids, which are useful for containing evaporation in recipes that call for long, gentle simmering. For this reason, sauté pans are also nicely suited to braises or any stovetop recipes that call for large amounts of liquid.

SILICONE BAKING MAT: Used to line shallow baking pans when making foods such as cookies and pastries to prevent sticking. They can withstand high temperatures in the oven and can also be used in the freezer. Dough can be rolled out on them, and they can easily go from prep station to chilling to the oven. They are easy to clean and reusable.

STAND MIXER: A heavy-duty machine with a large bowl and various attachments used to mix, beat, or whip foods at varying speeds. Stand mixers are necessary for making heavy, dense, or stiff doughs for cookies or yeasted breads.

WOK: This versatile Chinese pan is ideal for stir-frying, deep frying, and steaming. Traditionally made of plain carbon steel, woks usually have a rounded bottom that allows small pieces of food to be rapidly tossed and stirred. It also has high, gradually sloping sides to help keep food circulating inside the pan during stir-frying. In Western kitchens, round-bottomed woks are held in place over gas burners by a metal ring that allows the flames to rise and distribute heat around the pan. Woks with flat bottoms help distribute heat more efficiently on electric burners. They are sometimes sold with a lid for steaming.

ABOUT THE AUTHOR

TARA THEOHARIS is the author of cookbooks including *Pixar: The Official Cookbook*, *Minecraft Gather, Cook, Eat! Official Cookbook*, and *Break an Egg!: The Broadway Cookbook*. She loves creating approachable recipes inspired by her favorite fandoms. When not experimenting in the kitchen, she can be found playing games and binging movies with her husband and sons in Seattle.

ACKNOWLEDGMENTS

First and foremost, I have to thank Jaclyn Trahanas for the initial idea for this book. And thanks to Rhonda Miller, Roni Theoharis, and Christine Zakhour for their assistance on brainstorming the movies to include!

Thank you to my own leading man, Alexander Theoharis. You make my life an adventure in all the best ways. Thank you for your support and guidance, and for taste-testing all of my recipes.

Thank you to Anna Wostenberg for editing this book and always encouraging me to come up with more puns.

And thank you to Drew Barrymore, Sandra Bullock, Reese Witherspoon, Julia Roberts, and so many more for creating the iconic and lovable characters we all grew up with. You make us laugh, cheer, and fall in love in every movie you do.

Finally, thank you, reader, for loving love, loving food, and wanting to combine those loves together. Now stop reading and get cooking!

INSIGHT
EDITIONS

PO Box 3088
San Rafael, CA 94912
www.insighteditions.com

Find us on Facebook: www.facebook.com/InsightEditions
Follow us on Instagram: @insighteditions

ISBN: 979-8-88663-718-2

Publisher: Raoul Goff
SVP, Group Publisher: Vanessa Lopez
VP, Creative: Chrissy Kwasnik
VP, Manufacturing: Alix Nicholaeff
Editorial Director: Thom O'Hearn
Art Director: Stuart Smith
Senior Editor: Anna Wostenberg
Editorial Assistant: Anna Friedman
VP, Senior Executive Project Editor: Vicki Jaeger
Production Manager: Deena Hashem
Senior Production Manager, Subsidiary Rights: Lina s Palma-Temena

Special thanks to Kristen Mulrooney for editorial contributions.
Photography, food, and drinks styling by Waterbury Publications

ROOTS of PEACE   REPLANTED PAPER

Insight Editions, in association with Roots of Peace, will plant two trees for each tree used in
the manufacturing of this book. Roots of Peace is an internationally renowned humanitarian
organization dedicated to eradicating land mines worldwide and converting war-torn lands
into productive farms and wildlife habitats. Roots of Peace will plant two million fruit and
nut trees in Afghanistan and provide farmers there with the skills and support necessary
for sustainable land use.

Manufactured in China by Insight Editions

10 9 8 7 6 5 4 3 2 1